Listen, Lord . . .

I'm tired of all the experts.

People who try to tell me how to raise my c n, how to run my marriage, how to be a better m, how to save the world.

I've listened to them far too often, been intimi d by them too often. I have underestimated my own-stincts and common sense—and you.

I am going back to the Bible for some good old-fsh-ioned guidance: "Honor thy father and thy mother." "Bring up a child in the way he should go and he will not depart from it." "Love thy neighbor as thyself."

Yes, and the Ten Commandments, and a whole lot more.

I'm going to rediscover this long-neglected gold mine, God. I'm going to see how it stacks up against the advice of today's so-called experts.

(And while I'm at it, I'm going to be a lot more careful about posing as an expert, myself.)

Who Am I, God?

The enthralling new bestseller by the author of
Love and Laughter
and

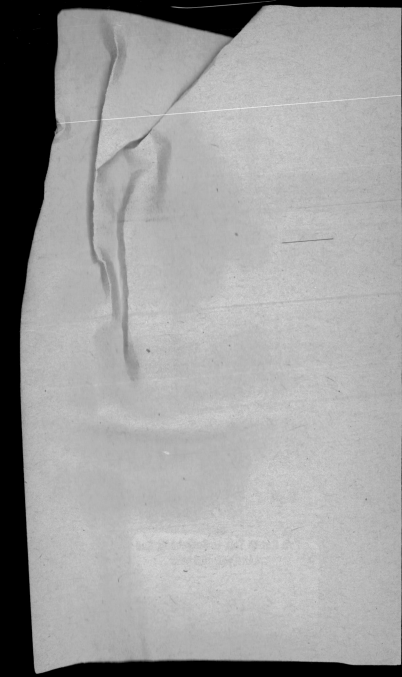

WHO AM I, GOD?

MARJORIE HOLMES

Illustrated by
BETTY FRASER

SPIRE BOOKS

FLEMING H. REVELL COMPANY

FOR EVELYN

WHO AM I GOD?

A Spire Book published by Bantam Books, Inc. for
The Fleming H. Revell Company by arrangement with
Doubleday & Company, Inc.

First Spire Printing May 1973
2nd printing
3rd printing

Contents

Who Am I?

I applied mine heart to know, and to search, and to seek out wisdom, and the reason of things.

ECCELSIASTES 7:25

Who Am I?

Oh, God, who am I? Where did I come from and where am I going? What am I doing here?

Sometimes, passing a mirror, I am startled by the stranger who seems to be wearing my face. Who is this person who looks like me (poor thing) and rushes around in my body?

She cleans up the kitchen, sorts the laundry, yells at children, loves, worries about and fights with a man who seems to be her husband.

She goes to bed at night, gets up in the morning, cooks, eats, gets other people off to their destinations and then hurries to her job. A job in a sometimes drearily familiar, sometimes startlingly strange place. Or a club where she knows almost everybody—and nobody, actually.

And we are the same person, this woman and I. Yet different, too—as if I am allowed to wake up sometimes in her presence and cry out: "Hey ... *you!* Who are you, and what are you doing here?" And she can only regard me, stricken and surprised.

Who am I? Who am I, God?

I am alive—I must be. See, I am shaking a hand: I can feel it warm against mine. I am conducting a meeting: I hear my own voice calling for the treasurer's report. I am racing to the car, gabbling with somebody; our heels click on the walk, the door bangs. I am hurtling along a highway to pick up a child and take him to Little League.

But in the very moment of awareness, I am sometimes pierced by the sheer pointlessness of all this.

2

What does it matter, God? What does it *matter* whether the clothes get sorted, the kitchen cleaned, the treasurer read her dull report? What would it matter if I didn't show up for work? Would the course of human events be altered in the least if my son didn't get to the ball game?

This woman who seems to be doing these things in my body, wearing the label of my name. What has she got to do with *me?*

Forgive me if this sounds frenzied, God. I *feel* frenzied—and frightened sometimes.

It's all going by so fast. Life's rushing past me, time is sweeping me along in its torrent, and I don't know where I'm going, or why. I long to grab something along the way. I can't slow it down, but I feel that I've got to grab something, hang onto something, or I'll be obliterated altogether. The real me (if there is such a creature) will be even more lost than she is now.

Already half-deafened by the demands of other people, half-blinded, desensitized, she will go down to death with her own needs not only unmet but only half-recognized.

Rescue me, Lord. Stretch out your hand to me.

I know you must be out there—somewhere. And if I can only find you, hang onto you, perhaps I can be saved. Not in the sense of an afterlife, but saved from the choking futility of this life now.

I am groping for you, God. Stretch out your hand—and don't let me fight you away. Draw me onto a place where I can at least get perspective. Where I can meet myself on quieter terms and try to figure out who I am, where I am going—and why.

The Outburst

I know this seems childish, Lord, but I'm so hungry for appreciation. I work and slave for everybody, but how often am I thanked?

I knock myself out to make the house lovely, but who notices? I clean and polish, arrange flowers, lug up wood for a fire, put some good music on the record player. But the hungry horde descends, throwing their things around, wrecking the whole effect, demanding to know when dinner will be ready.

I look up recipes, lavish care on something special, but they've stuffed themselves on snacks before they get to the table. Or they rush off someplace—they're not even there!

Or they sniff at it suspiciously and push it away; or gulp it without comment.

I cried when this happened last night, Lord. I made a fool of myself, rushed bawling from the table. They were all very contrite, but the damage was done. I'd made them feel ashamed, *obliged* to be nice to me instead of doing it sincerely, out of love.

I'm sometimes sick of the whole bunch, God. I want to get out, let them shift for themselves. (And come to think of it, maybe I should; a vacation might do us all good.)

Or I want to do something that will make them sit up and take notice. Make a speech, win a prize, get a promotion. Anything, almost anything, to make my family realize I don't exist solely for their convenience.

There. I feel better now. Thank you for listening to this outburst. It will help me not to go to pieces so easily again.

These Gifts, These Dreams

I've got to talk to you some more, God, about what my life's supposed to mean. For I'm troubled, Lord, tormented and guilt-ridden by the very abilities you gave to me.

The ability to reproduce, raise young—yes, yes, I thank you with all my heart for that. I am truly grateful, whatever the worries and sacrifices. Yet to "be fruitful and multiply" isn't considered noble anymore; it's downright irresponsible!

The world is begging us to cease, desist; it's being threatened by our very product. And even if this weren't so, would motherhood be enough?

Oh, God, dear God, what of the rest of me?

The talents you entrusted to me. The intense conviction that I was destined to use them in some effective and lasting way. Why did I have this first high fervor if it was only to end at a kitchen sink? Why those obscure yet vivid longings if they were not to lead to more?

I repeat—I am infinitely glad to be human, all woman, that I fell in love and joined my life with that of a very good man. And these children I've brought into existence—they were both to fulfill myself as a woman, and to send my own dreams on.

Yet these dreams, dear Lord, these dreams. Can anyone ever truly pass the torch of his dreams to another?

Isn't the gift and purpose you planted within each of us, man or woman, too special, too important for any substitute?

God, whatever these goadings may be, let me face up to them.

Bitter or sweet, give me the courage to know them for what they are, childish illusions or valid challenges. And to act on them.

Help me to know what to do about my life and my mate and my children. And about myself, not only in relation to them, but to me ...

And to you. And the reason for which you created me.

The Vital Self

Listen, Lord, please listen ...

This woman is in a state of depression that is almost suicidal because her husband has left her. Help her, comfort her, but oh, shake some sense into her too.

Make her realize that life still has significance. Self still has significance.

I don't think you meant any of us to become that immersed in another human being, whether it be husband, wife, lover, parent or child.

It devalues the precious self that you created. It even devalues the other person, for it imposes too grave a burden. It makes him nothing but the bearer, supporter and source of comfort and identity for oneself.

Lord, give my friend the strength to stand up and reclaim herself as a person. Her own vital dignity and individuality.

As for me, when I ask, "Who am I?" don't let the answer ever depend on somebody else.

To Tell The Truth

I'm tired of trying to be so many people, Lord. Trying to please and guide and fulfill the demands not only of my own family but of the world.

Even though he's kind and helpful and doesn't say much, I know my husband wishes I ran a perfect house like his mother (who really didn't have much else to think about). Or a lovely, artistic home like some of our childless friends. Yet all this with a houseful of children; all this while I'm trying to help *pay* for the house.

I'm also supposed to raise flowers like so many of our neighbors, maintain a beautiful yard. And to be a good hostess, cook gourmet meals, entertain as often as we're invited out.

I can't keep up with all this, God, and I feel guilty that I can't.

The children expect me to hear their problems at any hour of the day or night. I'm supposed to be all-wise, all-powerful, a kind of human computer: Punch her and she'll emit instant solutions.

My church and my community almost coerce me to

pitch in. Teach a class, conduct a drive, write letters to Congress. They make me feel guilty when I refuse.

Even when things go wrong with the world it's somehow my fault: I didn't vote right (or vote at all). "We are all to blame," I'm told, for racial injustice, for violence, for war.

Lord, I'm confused and wearied by these roles. I can't be an expert in so many fields (I can't even be efficient!), and I'm sick to death of trying.

Their very number has clouded my perspective. I don't know what's important, what is supposed to be my overriding purpose. I don't know *who* I am—wife, mother, homemaker, hostess, professional, public servant or what.

It's like the TV show *To Tell the Truth*. Will the real *Me* please stand up? If somebody asked that question, I wouldn't know who would rise.

Lord, help me to sort out all these roles and make some sense of them. Help me to find the person you really want me to be, and to be true to that self.

Recognition

How desperately we women are seeking recognition, God.

Holding office in church or community or clubs. Heading committees, drives, good works.

We are doing this because we want to serve, there's no denying that. But you know, how well you know, a lot of this is also escape. A frantic escape from the thankless job of running a house, from the tasks that seem to lead nowhere, from the people who take us for granted.

We want to be thanked for our efforts, even if the thanks comes only from each other. We want to be praised, we want to hear some applause. We want to get our names and our pictures in the paper.

It is proof that we are somebody in our own right; the blind maw of the family has not swallowed us whole. We exist.

And this is vital to us, God. We must have this reassurance.

It is not vanity that drives us on this hectic route; it is a kind of affirmation that the life you gave us is significant.

Thank you for planting this very real need in women. Our search for recognition helps to get the world's work done!

The Simple Step

Thank you, God, for helping me to cut through my own confusions, arousing me from my own stupid lethargy. For showing me that I must stop bewailing my circumstances and do something about them if I would be free.

Thank you for these courses that are both available and inexpensive. And for the fact that I finally woke up to them.

Thank you that my husband is understanding, and so are the children. Actually proud that Mom has some interest in life besides their achievements and their needs.

Thank you for these opportunities—to listen, to learn, to find my mind waking up again. For the challenge that I'm forced to face—to put up or shut up about my so-called abilities. So that when I've finished I'll know that either they were worth the self-flagellation or something better forgotten. So that at least I'll be mentally free.

Thank you for these teachers. This fellowship. This stimulating talk. This atmosphere of getting back to college, the place where the spark of ambition is kindled in so many of us, and the dreams can seem so near.

And oh, Lord (though I hope this won't happen), even if I find the dream unattainable or not worth the candle, I know I'll be a fuller, deeper person for this experience.

Happier in my role as a wife, and a better mother to my family.

The All-Purpose Person

Suddenly, but sincerely, I want to thank you for making me an all-purpose person, God.

Today, out of a blue sky almost, came this joyful awareness of authority, ability and strength. This acute consciousness of the sheer wonder of being needed by so many people. And of being able, however faultily, to meet so many demands.

Thank you that I could get up early to take my

husband to the airport. That when I got home the phone was ringing; even though it's Saturday, the office needed me.

Our daughter announced that she had to have a present for a birthday party. Our son was having complications about getting title to the car he's working for.

Somehow I managed to resolve these problems and still get to my job. I felt like a smooth-running elevator, lifting people to levels they couldn't reach without me. And I enjoyed it, Lord!

Now I'm cooking dinner for some friends whose husbands are also away. I bought some flowers, started a crackling fire.

And I feel again the surge of joy that came to me this morning. A sense of—*totality*. Not of being splintered and weakened as a person, which I bewail so often. But of being added to by the very diversity of my roles.

I realize that you never give me more than I can do. And that these multiple demands are not meant to tear me apart but to add dimension to me. To make me whole!

Thank you for this knowledge, God.

Who Are My Children?

One generation passeth away, and another generation cometh.

ECCLESIASTES 1:4

The Lovely Aliens

Oh, Lord, please bless these lovely aliens, my children.

They seem so strange to me at times, not even resembling me in face or traits or body.

It is sometimes hard to believe that I had anything to do with producing them, these vigorous strangers going their own way with such vigor and independence.

The fact that I even clothe and care for them seems an anomaly, as if I am just some loving outsider attending their needs.

At times I protest this, Lord. I don't want to be an outsider.

I am lonely for the deeper attachments we had when they were small. I feel a hungry desire to know more truly what they think, to share their lives.

A kind of righteous indignation rises up, demanding, "See here, if it weren't for me you wouldn't *be* here! Pay attention to me, draw me in. Darnit, I'm your *mother*."

Then I am reminded of my own blithe, often inconsiderate youth.

You help me to see that this is nature's way, however cruel, of cutting natal strings. I cannot carry them forever in my womb, or on my lap. (Only in my heart.)

The burden of it would be intolerable. For my sake as well as theirs, I've got to let them alone, let them go.

So bless them as they make these fierce, sometimes

foolish, sometimes faltering strides toward independence. Give them strength—they're going to need it!

Don't let my self-pity sap their progress. God bless these lovely aliens, my children.

Teach Me
To Talk To Them

Please teach me to talk to my children. With patience, good humor, sympathy and understanding (insofar as it is *possible* for an adult to understand his children).

And teach me to listen to them in a way that will make them want to talk to me.

I am so often baffled by the things they say, shocked by the expressions they use. It sometimes upsets me to know they have the ideas they express.

Then I realize that this is the only way we can hope to bridge the differences between our generations. This frank, free exchange of thoughts.

Help me to keep my emotions out of it, Lord.

Don't let me get my feelings hurt; don't let me get mad. Keep me from sentimental comparisons (how much harder we had things at their age, how respectful and considerate we were of our parents). Guard me against faultfinding and accusations of ungratefulness.

Oh, God, teach me to talk to my children with tact and common sense.

Let me be open to their arguments; don't let me pretend to know all the answers. Let me be honest

with them. Don't let me compromise my values. But
don't let me be arrogant either. Don't let a desire to
be right dominate my desire for genuine communica-
tion.

Let love, genuine love, pervade our conversations.
Let laughter give it joy and flavor.

Lord, teach me to talk, and to listen, to my children
so that they will always want to come back.

Give Them Pride In Self

Please give my children pride in self.

Not pride in background, pride in money or position. But only pride in self.

Whenever they would hunger too avidly for popularity, whenever they would compromise their values—say things they don't mean, dress to please, walk
and act and think to please, to belong—remind them,
oh God, of this:

The incomparable value of self.

Help them not to cheapen and warp that self.

Not to risk its very survival by falsity and camou-
flage.

Help them to see (and me to help them see) that
popularity is fleeting. That people vanish and new
crowds must be faced.

That the frantic chasing after crowd acceptance or
adulation is the most exhausting, least rewarding of
any race.

Self can be obliterated in it, the precious integrity
of self.

God, give my children pride in self.

Not a pride that is vain, offensive or condescending, but aware of its own priceless individuality.

Let them value it, cherish it, fight for it if need be.

God, let my children respect the proud individuality of others. And give them a strong and honest pride in self.

For The Parents
Who Choose A Child

God, bless the little new life that has come into this home.

It is too young to wonder about itself yet. It laughs and cries and sleeps as all babies do. It reaches out its arms to be held, fed, comforted.

It doesn't ask, "Who are my parents?" It simply knows that it is loved and wanted—and therefore does have parents.

God, bless these parents who worked and waited so long for its coming.

Bless the room they have fixed up so tenderly for it, the plans they have for it, their apprehensions for it. And ease the secret apprehensions they have about themselves.

Help them to see that they are better prepared than many whose children are not always welcome. And that mere blood is no guarantee of love or wisdom.

Reveal to them the beauty of being adoptive parents. Or foster parents. For to adopt is to choose, voluntarily to accept the responsibility of an otherwise parentless child. To foster is to guide and encourage and care for, to cherish.

And let this lucky child of their adopting and their fostering comfort and cherish them, too. Bless the home they will have together, the family they will be.

And when any of them asks, "Who am I?" let the answer be, "You are mine and I am yours, and we are all God's children."

Let Them
Have Beauty Again

Oh, God, they have so brief a time to be young and beautiful with youth.

I grieve for the waste of that beauty. For the way they distort it, deny it, hide its very existence behind beards and hair and ugly glasses and ugly clothes.

Age and care and worries work their own ravages on beauty. These faces will be seamed and sagging all too soon. These bodies will thicken, have ailments, slow down.

How sad that this lovely time of firm skin, bright eyes, slim, supple bodies, should be deliberately brought to ruin, camouflaged.

It would be comical if it weren't so sad—these overgrown children, many of them arrogating to themselves the right to reform society, disguised and costumed in the stuff of a horror movie.

No wonder the world looks hideous to them!

I grieve for them, Lord. Their pathos, their confusion, their struggle to find themselves through the unnatural barriers of their own disguise.

I grieve for the way they have laid waste to their own brief beauty. A beauty that cannot come again.

Oh, God, please make our young people aware of how important beauty is. Please give their own beauty back to them.

Make Him Realize

Oh, God, dear God who created him in the first place, please help my blind, naïve, misguided child.

"I will go my own way," he says, "I will do my own thing. It's my body and my mind."

He's trying to find himself through sheer physical sensation. He's trying drugs to "expand his mind."

And I am sick with fear. My flesh goes rotten at the thought, my blood is water in my veins.

I am so staggered before this evidence and these words that I don't know where to turn.

Show me, please. Don't let me make a misstep, do something that would turn him against me forever or further damage his life.

Help me, help me, please.

But first—help *him*.

Let your mighty wisdom rouse his own intelligence before it's too late. Make him see that any artificial means toward self-discovery leads to the opposite of what he's seeking.

It is not self-assertion. It is submission to an unknown force beyond his self-control.

It is self-annihilation. It is self-*denial*.

Oh, God, please rescue my child from his self-destruction. Please make him realize its futility and its danger, and help him. Help him now.

Child In Trouble

My child is in trouble, deep trouble, God.

I come to you weak and limp from sheer alarm. I fall to my knees before you.

I am almost too dumb with disbelief to articulate this problem. You know the details all too well, and so I shall spare myself and you a wild recital.

But oh, dear God in heaven and upon this earth, please support me in this hour of trial. And support my child.

Lift us up, get us back on our feet. Don't abandon us; don't let us lose our common sense, or our faith in you.

What has happened can wreck many lives if we go to pieces and forget that you are standing by, ready to guide us if we will let you.

Ready to comfort us. Ready to help us through the difficult hours that lie ahead.

You, who are in the very breath and substance of each of us, including the tragedy of this child—let us feel your presence.

Fill us with your peace, your assurance of a right solution.

Let us feel that blessed presence now, and trust in your love, which will see us through this deep trouble with our child.

Deliverance

Oh, God, my child has been delivered from the terrible trouble we faced. Thank you.

We have all been spared some of the dire complications we feared. And we are thankful, oh, so thankful.

Though we went through hell for a while, we came through safely. You gave us the courage we needed, you gave us the understanding.

You gave us the faith we had to have—in our child, in ourselves, and most of all in you.

Now that the worst of it is over, let us all pause for a moment to renew our forces before you. Let us hang onto that understanding and that courage and that faith—in the good times as well as the time of trouble.

Help us all to keep closer to each other—and to you.

Help us to be able to talk more freely to each other—and to you.

If we can do this, if that is the only lesson we have learned, then all our suffering will have been worth it.

Thank you for what we have gained from this experience.

Thank you for delivering us from our terrible trouble.

I'm Tired Of All
The Experts

Listen, Lord . . .
I'm tired of all the experts.
People who try to tell me how to raise my children,
how to run my marriage, how to be a better person,
how to save the world.

I've listened to them far too often, been intimidated
by them too often. I have underestimated my own
instincts and common sense—and you.

I am going back to the Bible for some good old-
fashioned guidance: "Honor thy father and thy
mother." "Bring up a child in the way he should go
and he will not depart from it." "Love thy neighbor as
thyself."

Yes, and the Ten Commandments, and a whole lot
more.

I'm going to rediscover this long neglected gold
mine, God. I'm going to see how it stacks up against
the advice of today's so-called experts.

(And while I'm at it, I'm going to be a lot more
careful about posing as an expert myself.)

The Friendless Child

She thinks nobody likes her, Lord. And right now
she doesn't have many friends.

She's a late-bloomer. She's going to be poised and lovely someday, but that's small comfort for the awkwardness and anxiety now. ... Waiting for the telephone to ring. Not having anybody to walk with at school, or to sit with at lunch.

I know that's why she's sick so often: she dreads going. And I feel cruel that I must force her; my heart is ripped to ribbons, for there are sometimes emotional battles.

Seeing her go drooping down the walk, I could cry—and often do. You know how my prayers for her simply ache in me all day.

But now, Lord, I'm praying more specifically. If any of this is my fault, forgive me, and help me to make amends:

If I've neglected any talent or longing that could be developed to give her confidence, guide me to the proper sources. To congenial people who will see her potentials, draw her out.

Thank you for this direction, Lord.

If I've been too busy with my own activities to do justice to her social life, show me. Maybe I could do more about her having parties. And is this truly a home where she is always free, and proud, to bring friends?

If I've allowed her to be at a disadvantage in any way, through hair or teeth or clothes, show me that too. Give me the time and money and common sense to do what I can for her.

Lord, have I set her a good example in my own relationships? Have I demonstrated that to have friends we must be friendly? That we must not be hypercritical or touchy, that we must think of others instead of being self-absorbed?

And in my dealings with her, God, if I've been too critical or too concerned, too indulgent or too careful, if I've competed with her or humiliated her, or shown disappointment in her—or erred in the countless ways it's so easy to err in raising a child—well, forgive me and help me to improve.

But now, having searched my soul and resolved to do better, please release me. Help me to stop worrying about my daughter.

Help me to remember that the ability to attract people, be comfortable with people, is often a long and painful growth-process. And that parents can seldom provide shortcuts the way we can provide orthodontists and dancing lessons.

We can simply teach our fledglings to fly as best we can, and not let them cower in the nest. Make us realize that we can't spare them hurts, only provide love and encouragement.

But oh, dear Lord, whose eye is on the sparrow—please help my poor little bird. Lead her, as swiftly and wisely as possible, to the happy company of worthwhile friends.

I know that you will. Even today as I pray, good things for her are beginning. Thank you, God.

Give Them Goals

One of the most important things I can ask you, God, is to give my children goals.

Help them to want to "be somebody" in the most old-fashioned sense of the term. Give them the desire to make something of themselves.

Show them that the self with its individual gifts, large or small, is too precious to be diverted from its purpose by mass sneering at status, mass screaming about social values, instead of coming to grips with personal goals.

Lord, bless their sincere compassion and concern. But don't let them hide from their responsibility to become somebody, in the smokescreen of mob marches and mob rule.

God, open our children's eyes to the achievements of this society as well as its failures. Give them some awareness, some appreciation for the tremendous distance we've come in a very short time.

And let them realize that the only way to make it better is not by tearing down the old but by building up the new, through individuals bent on individual goals.

Show them how vital it is to the whole scheme of life to *be somebody*. Only the doctors, with your help, can heal the sick, the engineers build the bridges, the teachers teach.

Dancers, musicians, technicians, the people who heat the houses, fly the planes—each should have his right to be somebody, and so to serve.

Help them to see that each of us must first make something of himself before any of us will be able to make a better world.

God, give my children goals.

My Child
Has Lost Faith

My child has lost faith in you, God, and my heart is sad.

I hear him using all the familiar, well-worn arguments that deny your very existence. And I want to laugh and I want to scold and I want to cry.

For I remember far too well my own young voice of arrogance and inflated learning, dismissing you. And I see my mother gazing at me with the same expression I must be wearing now.

Only more hurt, more deeply disturbed, saying, "I can't answer your logic. I can only say I *know*."

I remember all the years I kept her waiting, hurt her, rejected her, condescended to her as I stormed and stumbled along all the enticing, argument-cluttered paths to find a faith that she had never questioned.

Waiting for a time when I would exclaim, "Why, it's true! I know."

And now I see my child kicking aside the foundations, setting off on the identical stormy journey. And I can only ask you not to lose sight of him. Not to let go of him altogether. And wish him a safe return.

Wish for the time when (I hope it won't take him so long) he too will say, with an air of discovery and relief: "I know."

What The Young Are Searching For

"There is no God," our sons and daughters say, heady with their new-found intellectualism and social consciousness. "Religion is just superstition."

Then they get out their ouija boards. Their books

on witchcraft and the occult. They light candles and attempt séances. They exchange tales of the supernatural. They avidly read their horoscopes.

In how many strange and diverse ways they demonstrate their need of you. Down how many mystical paths their young hearts go hungering.

Bless them, Lord, have patience with them. (And help *me* to have patience.) They are really hunting you.

They Say It's Serious

They say it's serious, God. They say our child can't live.

I am too broken by this news to make much sense.

I am too numbed and stricken to be brave with you. I've got to be brave for so many other people, so comfort me, Lord. Sustain me. Give me strength.

Don't let me cry out in bitterness against this verdict. Just help me to accept whatever higher, wiser verdict I must accept.

My heart implores you for a miracle, Lord.

Yet my heart also tells me that whatever miracles even you perform can only come from—goodness.

The wisdom and skill you have given doctors ... That is goodness.

The goodness and love of those who are praying for this child.

The pure human goodness of my own patient, cheerful, suffering child.

A vast fund of God-created goodness, from which

all healing comes. And from which we all must draw
our faith, our hope, our help.

I affirm and claim that goodness now, for my child.
I claim its power to make him beautiful and whole.
As he was in the hour of his coming. As he will be in
the hour of his return to you, whenever that is.

I claim its power to restore us, keep us whole, all of
us.

These Wonderful Kids

Thank you, Lord, for these wonderful kids.

Bless their fine young bodies that play tennis and
football, that dance and run and skate and swim.

Bless their hands that reach out, not with clenched
fists to strike and defy, but open to help.

When they go into the ghettos it isn't to incite and
destroy but to work. They paint, plaster, scrub floors.
They tend the sick, do the most menial jobs in hospitals, simply because they care. They coach and tutor
and counsel in camps for children whose parents can't
pay for camps.

And they work in their churches. I see them serv-
ing at the altar or marching down the aisle with the
choir. I see them conducting classes, waiting tables at
church suppers, washing windows, raking leaves.

Wherever I look I see them, Lord, these clean and
fervent kids.

If I don't see them I am looking in the wrong
places.

They are in organizations like the Scouts, the 4-H

clubs, the Ys. Still in track meets and basketball tournaments. Their ham radios call across the world, bringing cheer and sometimes rescuing lives. They climb mountains, explore the seas. They are still in schools and colleges.

Whenever I would despair of this generation, I have only to look about, go to one of these places, and have my faith restored.

Thank you that there are still so many of them, Lord. Kids who are reading, studying, working, practicing, getting an education. Kids who do not abuse their bodies, who are making the most of their minds. Kids who know pretty much who they are, and where they plan to go.

They are made of tougher stuff than we were, God. (They have to be, to survive.) They know more, care more, and are going to achieve more for mankind.

Thank you, Lord, for these wonderful kids.

A Child Leaving For Foreign Lands

Our daughter is packing her bags, God, for her first trip to foreign lands.

Bless her, keep her enthusiasm high (and my own nervous apprehensions safely hid).

Thank you for this wonderful opportunity for her. Thank you that you will help her to be equal to all its challenges. Give her courage, Lord, give her judgment, give her wisdom beyond her years.

Bless the people she will travel with, and the others she will meet. Help her to learn from them as they will learn from her.

Let your love shine through all her new relationships, warming and blessing them, so that only good will come of this venture. Joy and understanding, and lives forever enriched.

Keep her safe, Lord, wherever she is. Keep her well.

Stay very close to her so that she doesn't get too lonely or homesick or discouraged. (But don't let her get too busy to keep in touch with us.)

We love her so much, Lord, and she will be so far away from us. Take care of her for us, this daughter who is leaving for foreign lands.

He Was So Young

He was so young, God.

So young and strong and filled with promise. So vital, so radiant, giving so much joy wherever he went.

He was so brilliant. On this one boy you lavished so many talents that could have enriched your world. He had already received so many honors, and there were so many honors to come.

Why, then? In our agony we ask. Why him?

Why not someone less gifted? Someone less good? Some hop-head, rioter, thief, brute, hood?

Yet we know, even as we demand what seems to us a rational answer, that we are only intensifying our grief. Plunging deeper into the blind and witless place where all hope is gone. A dark lost place where our own gifts will be blunted and ruin replace the goodness he brought and wished for us.

Instead, let us thank you for the marvel that this boy was. That we can say good-bye to him without shame or regret, rejoicing in the blessed years he was given to us. Knowing that his bright young life, his many gifts, have not truly been stilled or wasted, only lifted to a higher level where the rest of us can't follow yet.

Separation? Yes. Loss? Never.

For his spirit will be with us always. And when we meet him again we will be even more proud.

Thank you for this answer, God.

Seeing Them Off
To College

Listen, Lord, please listen ...

I know now how my mother felt, seeing her children off to college. I think I understand the look in her eyes, the fear in her heart, the passionate imploring:

"Keep them safe. Don't let them be hurt too much. Let them make it, somehow."

For our getting there at all was a matter of jobs and scholarships and sheer blind faith.

Thanks to that faith, we made it. And have been richly blessed. Our children don't have to work or apply for scholarships.

But today there are far worse things to put that look in parents' eyes, that fear in our breasts: Drugs and liberal sex. Racism. Violent rebellions.

Seeing each of them off by car or plane or train, I too implore: "Keep them safe. Don't let them be too hurt. Let them make it, somehow."

For A Daughter About To Be Married

Listen, Lord, please listen ...
I am very conscious of you as I stand beside my daughter's bed. She is tired from all the preparations; she has turned in early. But I can't sleep. I have slipped in to tuck up the covers about her one more time. And to just stand here a moment absorbing her loveliness.

Tomorrow she is to be married—this baby that came to us at such an inconvenient time.

I know you have long since forgiven me for how dismayed and resentful I was then. I know you have been with us since, sharing our almost passionate pride and pleasure in her accomplishments. (You heard my thanks, you know my sense of blessing.)

You have been close to us too in the times of anguish, the illnesses, the arguments, the problems. (You heard and answered my prayers.)

Now I want to thank you once again for all those years that she has been a part of our family and has meant so much to us.

Bless her tomorrow as she stands beside the young man who is her final choice. Be with her as she makes her solemn promises. Stay close to her as she begins this new life that is her own, separate and apart from us.

Give her joy and pride in her husband; and him in her.

Lord, I could ask so many things for both of them. I could ask that you spare them trials, hardships, differences, sorrows. And I do ask that—yes, I suppose, even knowing that they will have their share.

Now I ask only that the companionship surpass the conflicts, the happiness far outweigh the hurts. And that whatever they face, they both stay close to you.

And oh, yes, one final thing, Lord, as I tuck her in this last time and turn away: May every child she bears bring her the delight that she has brought to us.

Don't Let Me Cry At The Wedding

Oh, Lord, don't let me cry at my little girl's wedding.

Don't let me cry as she comes down the aisle.

Let the radiance she has given our lives shine on my face now, to match the radiance on hers.

Let her feel, not my aching sense of loss, but my joy that she has found so fine a man to take care of her for us.

Oh, Lord, don't let my husband hurt at our daughter's wedding.

That arm that she's clinging to as proudly, trustingly, as when she was a little girl—thank you for it.

Let this be truly a moment of communion for them, a happy summary of all their memories as father and daughter.

Thank you for the steadiness of his step and the pride in his eyes as he gives her away.

Thank you for his smile as he takes his place beside me. For permitting us to come to this hour together, surrounded by so many people dear to us, to witness this beautiful ceremony.

My heart is full of thanksgiving. Almost too full of wonder and blessing. I love her so and rejoice so for her.

Lord, don't let me cry at my little girl's wedding.

For A Son Being Married

For little boys who grow up to be men, thank you, Lord.

For sons who cling to us when they're little and make us want to cling to them when they're grown, thank you, Lord.

For the troubles they cause and the triumphs they bring, thank you, Lord.

For the times when we despair of their ever amounting to anything, and the times when we're sure their brilliance will change the course of the world, thank you, Lord.

For the girls they love and lose, and the girls who love them, thank you, Lord.

For the wonderful girl who, incredibly, decides she wants to gamble her whole life on that of any woman's son, thank you, Lord.

For the high-flown plans these two are making, for their ambitions, their wise and their foolish dreams, thank you, Lord.

For the burdens he is willing to assume for her, and for the sacrifices she is willing to make for him, thank you, blessed Lord.

For this moment of music and flowers and awe when their lives are being joined for better or worse, thank you, Lord.

For the peace in my heart, along with the memories, the touch of pain and loss, thank you, Lord.

For their running so freely and joyously down the steps, for the rain of rice and good wishes, for the look of tender benevolence on all the faces about us, thank you, Lord.

And for the new life that they are beginning, this new home that they are creating, thank you, oh thank you, and bless it, gentle Lord.

The Child Who Doesn't Want A Wedding

God, I simply don't understand it, however hard I'm trying to: that these young people don't want to be married in the traditional way.

Are they right, God? That the money for a wedding could be better spent. That the ceremony itself in the presence of other people would be pretentious, a display of something too precious and personal to be shared.

It is, as they insist, their lives. And I echo the question they make so plain: What right have I to interfere? Yet something (my own savage maternal selfishness, no doubt) insists that my life is involved, too.

When you've brought a child into the world and cared for it so long, you deserve some climax to that effort. Some pride. Some sense of celebration and ceremony.

I feel robbed, Lord. Cruelly discarded. And the hurt is compounded because I feel ashamed of feeling this way.

God, forgive me for whatever is unworthy about my misery.

Let your loving truth shine through: that two young people are striving to be honest. They simply want to commit their lives to each other privately, in their own way.

Lord, help me to understand and to accept this gracefully.

But be patient with me in this sense of something important lost. (And please help *them* to understand and be patient with me, too.)

First Grandchild

Thank you, God, that it's here, it's here, our first grandchild!

I hang up the telephone, rejoicing. I gaze out the window, dazzled and awed. "Just a few moments ago," he said. "A beautiful little girl."

She arrived with the sunrise, Lord. The heavens are pink with your glory. Radiance streams across the world.

The very trees lift up their branches as if in welcome, as if to receive her. And I want to fling out my arms, too, in joy and gratefulness and welcome.

My arms and my heart hold her up to you for blessing.

Oh, Lord, thank you for her and bless her, this little new life that is beginning its first day.

On Becoming
A Grandmother

So now I'm a grandmother, God, and I am truly grateful.

Awe fills me. A sense of excited achievement. I want to laugh, I want to sing, I want to go down on my knees.

I also want to cry. For sheer delight, yes, and for tenderness. But also just a little bit for me.

A part of me isn't quite ready to be a grandmother, God. A vain, silly, private-life-hugging part of me.

The very word sounds so final. Old. Smacking of rocking chairs and easy slippers. Of being shooed into a corner to bake the cookies, knit the mittens or merely dandle grandchildren on my lap.

And that isn't true anymore. Not for most women—and oh, God, don't let it be for me.

However I adore this grandchild and will love those to come, don't let me become too absorbed in it. Let me keep my own work, my own interests, my own identity.

(Come to think of it, everybody will be better off if I just keep on being me.)

And now that I've confessed my secret reservations, let me accept this new phase of my life proudly.

Grandmother . . . I will grasp and savor the true beauty of that word—its grandeur and its glory. To be a grand–mother. What a compliment. May I live up to it.

Thank you, God, for revealing the wonder of becoming a grandmother to me.

Woman and Woman

Who is she that looketh forth as the morning, fair as the moon, clear as the sun, and terrible as an army with banners?

SONG OF SOLOMON 6:10

When Women Cry
"Help!"

Listen, Lord, please listen ...
I get so impatient with women who keep crying "Help!" and then won't take it. Who'd rather beat their breasts about their pointless lives and wasted talents.

I get so impatient with my beautiful, vital, truly gifted friend. Bestir her, please; arouse her in a way the rest of us can't. Give her more courage, more self-reliance.

She is so frustrated; she continually bemoans the futility of her days. Yet she refuses to do what she could to give her life a sense of purpose and direction.

She's having an affair with her alibis, Lord. It's so much easier to make excuses (the time, the money, duty) than to put herself to the test.

Basically she's scared, God, worried about her qualifications. When we who care about her point out how these problems could be resolved, her true concern comes out: "But everybody else would be so much better than I am."

God, cure her of this cowardice. Show her this isn't necessarily so. And even if it were, personal fulfillment shouldn't be a matter of competing with others, only with oneself.

Help her, and all women, to realize that talents buried can never be unearthed by wailing and wringing hands. They require the hard work of digging (and seldom does anybody else find and sharpen and hand over the shovel).

And even brought to light, there is always the risk that they aren't as bright as we once thought. Always the possibility of disappointment and failure.

Lord, help my friend to face the truth: Does she want help, or only an audience for her misery? Is she willing to work instead of whimper? Rouse her, stir her, give her the courage to take a few simple steps to help herself.

Psalm For A Sister

I will lift up my eyes and smile as I give thanks for my sister. My radiant, complicated sister, who is more than a sister—who is my friend. (Blessed is the woman who has one like her, and thrice blessed if she has more than one.)

I will thank the good Lord that we were children together, sharing the same room and for years the same bed.

I am grateful for the memory of her small body warm against mine. I rejoice to remember our playhouses and paper dolls and plans. Our secrets and surprises. Even our quarrels.

I feel a deep and poignant longing for those days when we were girls together. Life-hungry, love-hungry, each fighting her own battle, yet supporting each other against parents and the world.

My sister, oh Lord, my beautiful sister, often maddening, always understanding, always fun.

Thank you for this woman who shares my parents, my past, my blood; who sees me whole—the beginning, long ago, and the person I am now. My sister, whose faults are so clear to me—and dear to me, just as my faults are to her. Yet for all our differences, and the miles that lie between us, we would still battle the world for each other.

I laugh for the joy of my sister, all the comedy, the gaiety. And I sometimes weep for my sister. I long to comfort her, to hold her close, as we held each other for comfort or for courage as little girls.

Dear God, please take good care of her, this sister I love so much.

Blessing
For The Uncongenial

Listen, Lord . . .

You know there are a lot of people I can't stand. Please help me to get over feeling this way about them—and bless them.

Bless the woman who irks me with her petty gossip. And the one who infuriates me with her prejudice.

Bless the one so obviously jealous that she will never notice anybody's children or possessions or accomplishments but her own.

Bless the one who's always superior and condescending, who can't or won't unbend. Bless the one who's simply got to dominate, do all the talking, hold the center of the stage. . . .

(There are quite a number of them, Lord—these are just a few.)

Bless their beings that you created, the blood that beats in their veins. But please change their outlook on life. Not just to suit me—but surely to suit a lot of other people, and to make them happier themselves.

And please change *my* attitude, so that I'll stop feeling my hackles rise before their faults.

Whenever I must encounter one of them let me remember this blessing I have asked for them and be fortified against antagonism. So that with love I can understand them better, and laugh a little at all of us. Your poor, scared, defensive, eager-to-be-important creatures, struggling to get along with each other.

Heart Friends

How generous is God that he has given me these few and special women who are the true friends of my heart.

How he must love me that he has let us find each other upon this crowded earth.

We are drawn to each other as if by some mystical force. We recognize each other at once. We are sisters of the spirit, who understand each other instinctively.

There is no blood between us, no common family history. Yet there are no barriers of background, or even age. Older, younger, richer, poorer—no matter. We speak the same language, we have come together in a special moment of time, and the sense of union we feel will last throughout eternity.

How generous is God that he has given me so many other women I can call friends. Dear, good, life-en-

riching women who add flavor, value, delight. I would
be the poorer without them.

Yet surely the Lord's true concern for us, his children, is to lead us to these rare and special few. The
ones who call out to us from the crowds, who hold
fast to us through trials, triumphs, long separations.

The friends with whom the heart feels joyfully at
home.

The Bargain Hunter

These bargains, Lord, all these lovely bargains!

I was so delighted to find things so reasonable, I
was so proud at how much I was saving. But now I'm
shocked and stricken at how much I've spent. (At
first, counting up, I thought there must be some
mistake.)

I can justify everything. (Well, almost everything.)
But thinking up the arguments and explanations, I
find misery replacing that first bright elation. Will I
really convince my husband, who's struggling to make
ends meet? What sort of dimwit will I seem to the
children, when I've been lecturing *them* about cutting
down?

Lord, this may seem a silly thing to pray about:
But please put my husband in a good mood. If
possible, about money. (A raise, maybe? A contract?
An unexpected refund on the income tax?) Anyway,
give him an extra measure of understanding for feminine follies. Especially at bargain sales.

And don't let the children think me too inconsis-
tent, please. Let them at least like what I got. Ap-

prove my taste if not my judgment, and maybe even agree that this shopping spree was wise. Lord, since there's no undoing this day's bargains, please let them prove to *be* bargains, if only in family forgiveness and kidding.

But please in the future help me to remember: When things seem so "reasonable," I'd better be a little more reasonable myself.

Gossip

Oh, God, deliver me from the sins of gossip. Malicious gossip—you know the kind I mean.

Gossip that lusts for the weaknesses of others, thrives on their real or supposed shortcomings, offers them up as a living sacrifice to be mutilated for the relish of idle tongues.

Not the other kind of gossip, God. The talk so dear to women—a lively interest in other people, their virtues and values and foibles. Surely you don't condemn or expect us to condemn ourselves for this human, so very female trait. (I don't think people who "never gossip" in this fashion are so noble; they just don't have the imagination to be interested.)

But cruel gossip, God. Talebearing gossip that can cause such needless pain, wreck friendships. Gossip without charity, gossip without any attempt at compassion or understanding.

Self-righteous gossip. Gossip that condemns, dares to judge.

Men are less prone to this kind of gossip than

women. Either they're too busy to be bothered or they're acutely uncomfortable when it occurs.

Not so women—and I am very much a woman. Please guard me from the very real sin of malicious gossip, God.

Psalm For Women
Who Serve The Lord

Who can surpass the beauty of women who do your work, oh, Lord? The beauty of their willing bodies and busy hands. The beauty of their character, their compassion, their sacrifices.

The husband of such a woman may protest at times, yet his heart is proud. He knows she is a happier person for it, a better mother, a better wife. For, like The Virtuous Woman of Proverbs, she does not neglect her own.

Though she may have toiled far into the night, she rises up early to care for her household. Then she is on her way. To schools and hospitals and churches, to ghettos and nursing homes.

"He that has eyes to see, let him see, and ears to hear, let him hear," we are told. How beautiful is the face of the woman who has both, for she sees and hears the need.

She visits the ill, the poor, the lost and lonely, those who are broken in body or spirit, whatever their age. They brighten at sight of her, they cling to her hand. She reads to them, writes for them, above all she listens to them. And her coming is often the one thing that gives them the courage to go on.

Or, a casserole in one hand, a Bible in the other, she gathers with others for sales and suppers and bazaars.

She has brought the fruits and flowers of her garden, the products of her kitchen and sewing machine. And the scent of these offerings is sweeter than incense; the music of pans and dishes and the voices of women working together as happy as any hymn.

Thank you for these wonderful women. They are angels in aprons, saints in station wagons. Surely they are beautiful in your sight, and blessed in the eyes of all who know them.

You have given the world no lovelier gift than women who serve you, Lord.

My Black Sister

Hear me, Lord ...

"Who am I?" I ask of myself, and life, and you. And if this is a critical question to me, how much more critical to my black sister.

I can trace my ancestors back at least a few generations. I claim this doesn't matter, I couldn't care less. I am myself, that's all.

But would I feel indifferent if my origins were slavery? If the dark people of my mysterious beginnings had been in chains? Wouldn't I too have inherited the chill weight of those chains?

And what if I bore the name of some white master who might or might not have been my grandfather. What then?

I must bring these thoughts to the surface. I must consider them as I search for my own identity. Let me remember my black sister, whose cry, "Who am I?" echoes through a deeper void and has a deeper note. A note of genuine agony.

I am grateful for this new awareness of my black sister, God. It will give me more understanding of her. More compassion for her.

It will show me new ways to help her break the chains. To walk with pride and independence. To become a whole person, able to say as I do: "I don't care. I am myself."

For A Husband's Mother

Did I ever think to thank you, Lord, for helping me choose a man who had a mother like this?

I hadn't the faintest idea how lucky I was then, but each day that I live I realize it more.

"Mother-in-law." "Daughter-in-law." The terms are both tender—and misleading. As if we're stuck with each other "by law," with all the rivalry, interference, and comic strip clichés those words imply.

When what we're really stuck with is our affection for each other, our genuine friendship; and the pride and love we both have for her son.

Did I ever think to thank you, God, that so fine a woman produced him and raised him to be so fine a man? (Though she could have done a better job in some directions, I only pray I'll be able to turn out husbands as good!)

Did I ever think to thank you for her skills at

cooking, sewing, keeping house? Skills she's always willing to share but doesn't try to force on me.

Or for her kind and clever fingers, always so busy, so lovingly making things for everybody else—children, grandchildren, people in need.

Did I ever think to thank you that she isn't perfect, Lord? (A man with a perfect mother would be impossible to live with.)

That she has faults like mine, off days like mine. But thank you that she is mostly patient, good-humored, and rich in common sense.

Thank you most of all that she is as glad to have me in the family as I am glad to be. That she knows I'm trying, with your help, to be a good wife to the man she brought into the world for me.

The Extra Commandment

There is this woman where I work, Lord, who is often curt and unkind. Or she simply acts so unpleasant, impatient, critical, that she upsets the rest of us.

We try to make allowances—at least a lot of us do. She is unhappy at home, we remind ourselves; she is probably going through the change of life.

But (and please forgive me) I think you should have given another commandment: "Thou shalt not hurt others needlessly. Nor let thy bad disposition disturb and add to the problems of other lives."

Lord, please bless this woman and ease her burdens.

But while you are at it, help her to see that the rest

of us don't always feel so good, that we have problems, too.

Mother

Dear God, how much you must have loved me to send me to this particular mother. This good and beautiful woman who was the source of me.

Because she lived, I live—and others live through me.

But now you have taken her back to yourself, and I am bereft. The hurt is intolerable. I want her as I did as a child when something went wrong.

I feel as if I must run through the world calling, "Mother, Mother, where are you?" as I ran crying through the house sometimes as a little girl.

"Here, dear, I'm right here," she would say, appearing. Or, returning from an errand, "My goodness, honey, I've only been gone a little while."

And now, even as I call out to her, I feel her presence.

It's as if she has put her arms around me as she used to, or is stroking my hair. And comforting, "Don't cry, honey, it's all right. I'm right here. You know I would never leave you alone for very long."

Thank you for this comfort, God.

The Woman Who Works For Us

God, bless the wonderful woman who works for us.

Who comes in so cheerfully to face our messes. Who brings order out of chaos, cleans up so faithfully.

Who is so good to our children. Rocks and cuddles the baby, visits with a daughter, scurries around to iron a shirt for a son.

Who shares our family's ups and downs as if they were her own. Who tells me her troubles and her joys.

Who sings hymns of praise as she scrubs a floor, who has never doubted your loving care despite the tragedies and deprivations she has known.

Who has raised decent, accomplished children who are a credit to this country. (I only pray ours will turn out so well.)

Our skins are not the same color; our backgrounds are totally different. Yet I love her, Lord, as I know she loves me.

Thank you that we enjoy each other, respect each other, and that you sent her to me at a time when we needed each other.

God, bless and keep this wonderful woman who works for us.

Liberation

Oh, Lord, have mercy upon all your liberated
women.

Pill-liberated from pregnancy and even most of the
miseries of menstruation. Law-liberated from having
unwanted babies when the pills go wrong.

Law-liberated too from a lot of the inequalities of
dealing with men. But suffering, nonetheless.

Crying, "Independence," yet pleading, "Comfort
and care for me," in the same breath.

Enslaved, perhaps more than ever, in the blind
confines of self.

Self-indulgence. Self-seeking. Self-searching. Strain-
ing to find some meaning to this rat race of being a
woman in a world where evil continues to triumph,
and there is no outer or inner peace.

For what pill can conquer the conscience?

What laws can liberate us from anxiety, frustration,
or our own self-contempt? Or the awful goads of
ambition, competition? Or the anguish of feeling
empty, futile, unappreciated, unloved?

Liberate us from our awful loneliness, Lord. Free
us from our confusions. Release us from our passionate preoccupation with self.

Liberate us from the bitter by-products of our very
liberation!

We have become crude with liberation, Lord. We
have lost more than we have gained. Our very freedom has only intensified the rat race and made the
evil more profound.

For we have compromised with evil, we have reproduced it, fed it at our breasts.

We have challenged man, "the enemy," and only become ridiculous and shrill, lacking both masculine dignity and feminine gentleness.

We have lost our innate *nobility*, somehow.

God, save us. Restore us to graciousness.

Make us aware once more of the sheer wonder and power of being a woman. Your assistant in creation and surely your assistant still in helping to create a fairer, surer, less chaotic world.

Take away our dependence on pills and laws. Let us stand on our own feet, beautiful and confident and proud. Women who set high standards once again. Women who set noble examples. Women invincible because we have earned respect and love.

That is the true liberation, Lord. Not only to be free to love but to be worthy of love.

Lead us to that freedom and that love.

The Working Woman

A time to rend, and a time to sew; a time to keep silence, and a time to speak.

ECCLESIASTES 3:7

Why Do I Want
This Job?

Listen, Lord, please listen ...

Help me to understand my reasons for wanting to take this job.

Is it really more money, the desire to help, to get ahead? Or is it the desire to escape? This house with its confusion, the incessant things to be done. The children. My husband. (For even though he's gone all day, alone with my thoughts, it's as if I'm still confronting him.)

Is it mainly my desire to stop feeling dull and inconsequential? Doing things nobody either praises or pays me for. Am I secretly seeking adventure—a change, a challenge that will make me feel important as a person again?

Listen, Lord, please listen ...

I know that my motives are a mixture of all these things. Help me to sort them out and weigh their separate values.

When it comes to money, don't let me forget the expenses. Clothes and carfare, baby-sitter, lunches, hairdos ... Subtracting all these, how much will my time away from home actually be worth? (And even though needing money causes problems, help me to remember that *having* more money can also cause problems.)

As for escape—I know there are women who feel trapped in offices, too. That whatever I undertake, there will be routine, repetition. And though I'll get a paycheck, I may not always feel important, or even appreciated.

God, give me the good sense to see the realities of this decision. Help me to put things in proper perspective.

If I do take this job, let me do so affirmatively, believing in its opportunities but not expecting perfection.

If I don't, guard me against regrets. Help me to bring some of the qualities I've just mentioned into the job I already have right here at home.

Thank you for listening to my perplexities and guiding me, God.

The Paycheck

Thank you, God, for this paycheck.

It isn't the amount that amazes me—simply the fact that I earned it. It bears my name. It is as if a small yet important slice of me has become tangible. An unseen part of myself has been minted—my mind, my talents, the work of my hands, my time.

This check also represents sacrifice. I had to give up other things to get it. And other people had to give up, too—some part of their claim on me.

Now, as I hold this check in my hand, let me thank you for all the things it represents. And ask that you bless it to its proper use.

I am glad that most of it will go to help the family.

Clothes, a piece of furniture, a payment on the car. But oh, don't let it just be buried in a blind bank of bills. (It is this need to see tangible results that drives a lot of us back to work.)

And suddenly, Lord, as I regard this check, I see the countless checks my husband has brought home so faithfully so long.

I wonder if I've ever thought to praise him for that vital piece of paper? Have I ever thanked him just for taking care of us? (Or a thousand other things nobody pays him for.)

Does he too feel a sense of achievement? Or a secret sense of protest and despair at the immediate melting of his earnings into the support of an indifferent family?

I don't believe it ever dawned on me until this moment that maybe men too would like to see some tangible results.

Thank you, God, not only for my pride in this paycheck—but for the insight it has given me.

This Day's Work

Lord, please bless this day's work.

The work that I will be doing, and the work that my husband does today. And the work of our children, at school and on their jobs.

Give each of us a sense of genuine interest and enthusiasm for it. Help us to be cheerful about it, even the parts of it we don't really like.

Help us not to become bitter and discouraged when

things don't go the way we want. Keep us from indifference or laziness. Help us never, under any circumstances, to cheat.

And may the work that we do today be worthy of our efforts. Something that helps rather than hurts. Builds instead of destroys. Work that makes some real contribution to the decency, comfort, wisdom and happiness of the world.

Lord, give us a sense of satisfaction at the end of this day's work.

Let us be able to look back on it, whatever its successes or failures, with pride; with the knowledge that it was worth doing and that we did our best.

Thank you, God, for blessing and guiding us through this day's work.

The Difficult Co-Worker

This man is so difficult to work with, God. So difficult I think sometimes I can't stand it.

Everything about him annoys me, upsets and repels me. And he must sense this, because whatever I do, I find him impossible to please.

God, we will never get anyplace until I overcome this feeling of active and intense dislike. So bless him.

Remind me that he is warm, living flesh and blood just as I am, with hopes and hurts and problems. That he has a home to go to—and people there who love him (right now I don't see how they can, but they do).

Whatever his faults, there are people who love him—as you love him, and as I must love him, too.

I sincerely pray that this will occur.

Bless the daily testing of my patience and will power in his presence so that I can overcome this aversion.

With your help I am going to find something in him to admire, and concentrate on that. With your help I am going to feel compassion instead of hate for the qualities I dislike.

With your help I will come to understand him, feel kindly toward him. In time, he may actually become dear to me.

Please bless this man who is so difficult.

The Coffee Break

Thank you, Lord, for this happy custom, the coffee break.

What comfort, the appearance of that little wagon and the fragrant pot that pauses at my desk. What pleasure this hot cup in my hands.

Even if I don't move from my place it reminds me that we are not simply cogs in a blind clanging machine. That somebody remembers that we are people, with bones that tire, throats that thirst, that life with all its labor is more pleasant when we can be refreshed.

And when I join the others it is even better. This time to talk, to get to know each other. To enliven the whole sometimes grim picture with comradeship.

So that when we go back to our tasks it is with a sense of something warm, not only in our veins but in our hearts.

Years ago this didn't happen. People worked all day without a halt, and the days were sometimes hateful, and always long.

I don't know who started the custom—maybe some efficiency expert. But whoever he was, bless him, and all those who have followed his lead.

Thank you, God, for this simple but dear and comforting thing, the coffee break.

Getting Ready
In The Morning

Please help me as I try to get ready this morning. Something important is coming up at the office, and I've simply got to be there.

But one of the children says he doesn't feel well. (Please don't let him have a fever; don't even let him try to get out of going to school by playing sick.)

Another has to have cookies for his class party. (Don't those kids ever do anything but eat?) I was too tired to bake them last night; I can put them in the oven while breakfast's cooking if you'll please just help me find some cookie mix.

Oh, Lord, I know I had a package—or was that the one the dog got into? My son will be so disappointed. And it'll be worse when I tell him I may not be able to get off in time for the program. (Only please do let

things work out so that I can—no last-minute dicta-
tion or long-winded clients I've got to be nice to.)

Lord, please don't let me get so harried by all this
that I overlook my husband. Remind me to tell him
where I put the clean shirts. (And please let him take
the one on top, which has all the buttons on—I
think.) And help me to remember his diet, that his
eggs have to be poached instead of fried.

I haven't got time to eat, God, just help me get
dressed. I pray that my good sweater is back from
whoever borrowed it last, and fit to wear, and that a
slip strap won't break or a stocking run. And that the
car keys will be where they're supposed to be, and
that the car will start.

Hang onto me through all this hectic confusion,
God. Help me to get everybody launched without too
many catastrophes, so that I won't feel guilty about
them. And so I can show up at my job looking
reasonably tidy and sane.

You've seen me through so many of these daily
crises, I know you won't let me down. Thank you,
Lord, for helping me get ready for work.

The Wonderful Boss

Thank you, dear Lord, for this wonderful boss.

He is direct, he is firm, he knows what he wants—
and expects it. But he is also considerate. He never
demands more of me than I am able to give. He is
genuinely concerned if he feels I am doing too much.

"Go home now to your family," he says. Or, "Take the day off, you've earned it."

He is meticulous, but he is never petty. He pays me the compliment of trusting my judgment about details. He knows he can rely on me; he not only says so, he shows it. And I rise to the challenge of that confidence.

He does not waste himself on empty flattery. But he is not stingy with praise. When he pays me a compliment I know he means it, and my joy and sense of achievement in the job I can do for him is fired afresh.

Thank you that he isn't perfect, God.

He is sufficiently human and faulty to keep me from feeling overawed. He can roar with laughter, he can lose his temper. But he doesn't make me or any of his staff the butt of his own disappointments and failures. He treats us as friends, fellow workers, without ever losing the authority we respect and love.

Lord, it's tough enough for a woman in the business world without having a tyrant or a childish rake for a boss. Right now I ask your blessing on all women who work and all the men who hire them.

May the men learn to become more like him, and the women be as lucky as I am. Thank you, God, for my wonderful boss.

Heal These Hostilities

There are so many conflicts and hostilities in this place lately, Lord, one almost has to duck. There are so many feuds and suspicions. It is as if poison had been released in the air.

Lord, please cleanse it. Let your infinite love flow through this room, here, now, purifying it.

Let your compassion, your forgiveness, your tremendous understanding begin to stir in everyone, deeply, strongly, rising up with such power it destroys every vestige of spite and unkindness.

Let the miracle of being alive, simply being alive and *able* to come to one place to work together, suddenly possess each one of us. Work its miracle of love and joy in us.

You created each of us. Your holy presence is in each of us. Release that presence now so that we may all be one.

Thank you for this healing, for this renewal of harmony and peace.

It's Been A Hard Day

It's been a hard day, God, and I'm so tired I can scarcely think.

Why do I do it? I wonder, closing my eyes as the bus lurches toward the next stop. Why am I here among these noisy strangers instead of home getting dinner for my family?

Why am I missing the sunset that I could see while calling them in? And how will I be able to manage all the things I've got to do when I get there?

I am discouraged, Lord, confused.

I can think of nothing sweeter than just staying home tomorrow cleaning cupboards and scrubbing woodwork. I could stop and nap if I wanted. I could call a friend, go out for lunch.

Yet here I am, grimy and exhausted after a day working for people who mean nothing to me. (And I've still got ironing to do tonight, and a PTA to attend.)

You know how delighted I was to get this job. How fervently I persuaded the others, and myself, that I must have it. But now I wonder. What am I really accomplishing?

This rushing around, this blind fatigue. Is it worth it—to me or anybody else?

Yet I'm ashamed to confess if I've been wrong. And afraid to quit! We've gotten used to the money. And what if I changed my mind and wanted to come back? They might not want me. And it would be doubly hard to start again.

Lord, thank you for telling me not to be too hasty. Not to try to make up my mind when I'm so tired and not yet home.

My stop is next—thank you. Someone will be there to pick me up (I hope). Maybe (oh happy miracle) somebody has started dinner, and if I'm lucky I might be able to use the tub.

When I'm fed and rested and the dishes are done, all this will seem less critical. If there isn't too much ironing, too much homework to supervise, if there aren't too many problems and the PTA doesn't last too long—well, maybe I'll be able to weigh sensibly the pros and cons.

For now, just for now—thank you for easing this sense of frustration and fatigue. . . . It's been a hard day, God.

Is It Fair To My Husband?

I sometimes wonder, Lord—is this work fair to my husband?

He knows that I want to do it; he encourages me in it. And he helps so much—around the house, with the children, looking after so many things to make it easier for me.

And that is partly the trouble. No matter how much I earn or contribute there is somehow this sense of guilt. Is it right that he do these things? Docs it deplete his sense of masculinity somewhat?

And the very money I make. Grateful as he is that it eases financial burdens, is it building a secret burden that may be worse?

Is it doing something to his pride? Is it a subtle affront to him as wage earner, provider, head of the house?

(Is it even possible that he could become like some men, dependent on the extra income, expecting a wife to work?)

Lord, I am confused about all this. Trying to talk it over with him doesn't help. He says no, of course not, don't be silly. But sometimes I think "he protesteth too much."

Please move him to be frank with me. And don't let me be too upset if the truth hurts.

Give us both guidance, Lord. If my work is hurting our marriage, please show us what to do.

He Doesn't Want His Wife To Work

You've just got to help this couple, God.

She's like so many women—she feels that her talents and training are not being fulfilled in running a home. But her husband is violently opposed to her going back to work.

He wants to be the sole provider, with all the old-fashioned male authority that comes from that role. He has little patience with her frustrations. "If you really loved me," he asserts, "you'd be willing to live on what I make. You'd be satisfied with your clubs and social life and me and the children."

And after years of seething or submission, she's fighting back. Threatening to defy him, to walk out and do it, no matter what.

Lord, calm them down; strike the goads of frantic self-interest from each of them and bring them gently together. Free them to talk to each other honestly but with a sincere desire to "understand, rather than to be understood."

Give him more perception of her needs. Show him that helping her to achieve the individuality she craves is as great an act of support as paying her bills, and in some ways more generous.

And help her to grasp his needs, too. His pride, his fears, his probable insecurity. And to be very tender and tactful about coping with those needs. Give her more appreciation; make her aware of the benefits as well as the drawbacks of his proud protection, and give her the grace to tell him so.

Help them to work out this problem, Lord. Give them the charity and compassion to compromise their differences.

Anyway, you've just got to help them. Except for this they're too right for each other to separate, but too miserable to go on.

Thank you for helping them, God.

Go With Me
To Work Today

God, please go with me to work today.

I am tired, troubled, discouraged.

There are so many problems at home, so many worries. Yet I must not carry them with me. I must be pleasant and poised, keep smiling. I must produce. I must earn my pay.

Thank you that you will help me. You will sustain me, sweep me free of these problems until I am able to think about them again, focus my entire attention on them.

Lord, I put my worries into your hands. I turn my family over to you now for blessing and safekeeping. I know that you will be with them, loving and directing them wherever they are, all through this day.

And I know that you will be with me.

As I go on with my work, I am suddenly thankful that I have it. I can lose myself in it, forget some of these problems. I won't be able to brood on them, and make the mistakes that come from idle brooding.

I can withdraw and get perspective. And when I return to all these situations in the family, I'll be better able to handle things.

Thank you for this reassurance. Thank you for going to work with me today.

For People
Who Work Together

Thank you, God, for the people I work with.

For their greeting in the morning and their good night when our work is done. For the sense of comradeship we have all day long. The gay ones and the cross ones, the sociable and the withdrawn.

Different though our natures, we meet for a common purpose, share common problems and pursue common goals. The strange and wonderful bond of a job to be done together makes us kin.

We are not "one big happy family," yet a family, nonetheless. We rejoice like a family, squabble like a family, have little feuds and alliances like a family.

We try to help each other, are genuinely concerned about each other. There is an affection between us that only people who work together can understand.

And sometimes when the day is over and we are parting to go our separate ways, wonder fills me at all these people I have come to know and love through work. They have added something priceless to my life.

Bless and keep them always, these people I work with, God.

How Much Do
The Children Need Me?

My children, Lord. I'm so mixed up about my children. How much do they really need me? And how much do I only think they need me?

Physically well cared for, are they suffering some deeper neglect that doesn't even show? Or am I only making excuses for a secret weakness in myself? The hurt that assails me when I realize how quickly they grow up, and how much I'm missing.

Sometimes, when our little girl waves good-bye, I can hardly stand it. I want to run back and scoop her up and say, "I'll stay home with you today." Whether she laughs or cries, there is this nagging sense of betrayal to her. And for me, personal loss.

Or a son calls me at the office with a problem. Too important, he thinks, to turn over to somebody else, too urgent to wait. Is this just a ruse to get my attention? I sometimes wonder inpatiently. Then guilt stings me. That wistful note in his voice ... If a son needs me, honestly needs me, what am I doing here?

Lord, help me to resolve these conflicts. So that if I go on working, it will be with a clear conscience.

Guilt and self-reproach are not only hard on me, they are certainly no help to them. If I must work, let me do so with enough confidence and self-respect that they will love and respect me for those qualities—and develop them in themselves.

Lord, I trust your loving wisdom to flow through this situation. I know you can help me resolve these conflicts between my children and my career.

The Blessings
Of A Working Woman

You have heard my self-lacerations, Lord, my doubts and my complaints. But right now I am filled with rejoicing. I want to count up the blessings of working:

What a blessing it is to have to get up and get going in the morning. To dress up, shape up, physically and mentally. The busy world has no time for my tears or tantrums. Instead of mourning my nonentity with other bored, self-centered women, I've got to prove myself out there.

And this is a blessing. For through it I am discovering my individual value, and so—identity.

I am grateful for the blessings (mixed blessings though they are) that this work has given my family.

I've learned to budget time more wisely. And though some things must be neglected, in many ways our home is more efficiently run than when I was there.

Thank you for this blessing. And for the children's developing self-reliance. Their cooperation. (They're doing things for me and for themselves they never did before.) This is an unexpected blessing. And so is the blessing of our growing harmony.

Maybe, being less absorbed in their problems, I can be more objective. Maybe my own enhanced self-respect gives them a new respect for me. Anyway, we laugh more, talk more, have more to share. Whatever the reasons, all this is a genuine blessing, and I thank you for it, Lord.

I see I haven't even mentioned the material things I thought I was working for.

These too are blessings—bills paid, luxuries we might not have had. But somehow these seem the least important of all. And if they ever become paramount or my desire for them disturbs the rest of it, please stop me, Lord. Don't let me go on pursuing false or foolish goals that would hinder my own soul's growth, or that of anyone dear to me.

Equip me with a dependable scale of values. Keep me always aware of the genuine blessings of my work.

Woman and Man

Who is this that cometh . . . this that is glorious in his apparel, traveling in the greatness of his strength?

ISAIAH 63:1

What Are Women
Doing To Men?

Listen, Lord, please listen ...

What are women doing to men, so many women crying, "Free us, give us independence, make us equals!" And what are women doing to themselves?

For the men are finally yielding. Some grudgingly, some protesting, some mildly amused, some simply gentlemen accustomed to granting a lady's wishes— they are making way for the fiercely determined women. Now we crowd their bars, invade their clubs, demand admittance to their most masculine professions. And are baffled that they still regard us with tolerance, amused dismay or secret contempt.

What are we doing to our men, oh God, what are we doing to our men? The men who still hunger to dominate but also to protect and take care of their women? Are we robbing them of their maleness? Are we turning them into eunuchs? Are we confusing them in their role as leaders, lovers, providers?

And what are we doing to ourselves?

Are we facing sexless lives with sexless men? How soon will we be expected not only to share the financial burdens but to become the providers? In demanding independence are we in danger of making the men dependent on us?

Oh, Lord, help us to realize our mistakes and get back into balance. Men and women are not the same. You didn't make us so, you didn't mean us to be.

You gave men strengths and skills and differences no woman can match. And you made women different, blessedly, wonderfully different from men.

Lord, please help us to find our true identity and self-expression without hurting, humbling, emasculating and making enemies of our men.

The Long Separation

We are facing a long separation, God.
Please give us strength, please give us courage.
We won't have each other to talk to at the day's end. We can't comfort each other. We can't hold each other when we are sick or tired—or filled with passion and joy.
We must learn to operate apart, in a world of strangers who don't care about us, or even friends who can't possibly care enough.

I can already feel the alarm just for his physical safety.
I can already feel the loneliness aching within me. Already sense the complexities, the problems.
Yet now, for now, dear God, let me thank you for the time we have had together. For the help we have been to each other, the lessons we've learned from each other and for the memories that will fortify us in the time ahead.

Bless him out there alone in the world fighting its battles for us. (Keep him safe, oh God, protect him.)
And bless me as I struggle along on familiar ground.

Don't let us feel sorry for ourselves. Help us to remember that you brought us together and will bring us back to each other.

And that meanwhile we can always talk to you and receive strength for this long separation.

For A Man Away

Oh, God, he's been away so long

You know how much I love him; you know how much I miss him. But you know too that sometimes it's hard to remember him—even how he looks!

There is this terrifying vacancy within me about him sometimes. As if he and our love never really existed: it was just something I dreamed. Even looking at pictures or rereading his letters can't quite bring it back.

Lord, what is happening to me during this long separation?

I am numb, my emotions deadened. I am not interested in other men, and for this I thank you, God. But sometimes I think it might be better if I were, if only to prove to myself that I am a woman alive, and capable of love.

I realize that this is wrong thinking, Lord.

Yet isn't there something false about being true when you're not even tempted? Rouse me from this awful torpor, please. Rekindle within me the *fires* of faithfulness, so that I am true from sheer loving choice instead of this deadly indifference.

Make my man vivid to me again—his voice, his face, the touch of his hands.

And, oh God, wherever he is, make me vivid to him.

Keep him faithful to me; don't let him grow cold and indifferent. Keep his love warm and vital too.

A Prayer For Fathers

God bless fathers, all fathers old and young.

Bless the new father holding his son or daughter in his arms for the first time. (Steady his trembling, Lord, make his arms strong.)

Give him the ambition and strength to provide for its physical needs. But even more, give him the love and common sense to provide for its hungering heart.

Give him the time and the will to be its friend. Give him wisdom, give him patience, give him justice in discipline.

Make him a hero in his youngster's eyes. So that the word Father will always mean a person to be respected, a fair and mighty man.

And God bless older fathers too.

Fathers who are weary from working for their young. Fathers who are sometimes disappointed, discouraged. Fathers whose children don't always turn out the way they'd hoped; fathers of children who seem thoughtless, ungrateful, critical, children who rebel.

Bless those fathers, Lord; comfort them.

And stay close to all these fathers when they must tell sons and daughters good-bye. When kids leave home, going off to college, or to marry, or to war—fathers need to be steadied in their trembling then too, Lord. (Mothers aren't the only ones who cry.)

You, our heavenly father, must surely understand these earthly fathers well.

We so often disappoint you, rebel against you, fail to thank you, turn away from you. So, in your infinite love (and infinite experience!) bless fathers, all fathers old and young.

The Teacher

This man, God. This wonderful teacher.

When I was young and scared and insecure you led me to him. Into his classroom, into my heart's true home.

For he was there. He fed me on riches I didn't know I was hungering for. He awoke my slumbering mind and made it sing. He taught me, he taught me!

This man, God, this great and good and beautiful man.

He cupped the little spark of my dream in his hands and blew it into living flame. He nurtured it, encouraged it, guarded it from going out. He never lost faith in me.

I worshiped him, Lord; he was my earthly god—and I know you understand. That you must have meant it to be.

For such a teacher is co-creator with you. He helps to shape a mind, a life, a destiny.

My teacher, my friend, the father of my spirit. Thank you, God, for this wonderful man.

The Heart Attack

I call upon the Lord in this hour of my dear one's heart attack. I ask for wisdom, speed, clear thinking.

Steady my fingers and my voice as I telephone for help.

Keep me in calm control as I minister to his suffering.

Help us both to realize that you are with us, holding my hand as I am holding his. You are in this room, filling it with calm and healing.

The rescue squad is here now. Thank you.

Bless them as they lift him gently onto the stretcher and maneuver it out the door. Thank you for their kindness and their skill as the ambulance goes crying down the street. (Surely they are blessed in your sight, these men who rush to the aid of others.)

Thank you for the clean white hospital bed. For the people who move so swiftly and confidently about to help him.

For the oxygen tank wheeled into this room, and the tent in which he lies sheltered now, away from me yet close to you as he breathes the precious stuff of life.

Lord, relieve his suffering. Thank you. Lord, let him know how much we all love him. Lord, give him peace of mind.

Lord, I believe in miracles, and I see his heart—that heart that he taxed and strained for so many others—growing stronger. Thank you. I see his warm red blood coursing freely through his veins. I see and claim these things for him through the power of your love.

Thank you for giving us courage and comfort throughout this heart attack.

The Man We Call Dad

For the man who gave me life, I thank you, Lord. For the wonderful man we call Dad.

For his joking, his eternal optimism, the joy he sheds, the friends he's always made.

For the home he provided for us. For the courage and determination with which he bucked the world for his family.

Dear Lord, for this father I thank you. For this wonderful dad.

I thank you for the lessons he taught us:

To be honest—never to take so much as a postage stamp.

To be brave—that so long as you did right you had nothing to fear.

To believe in yourself, because you're often the only one who will.

To be grateful, to appreciate little things. A bucket of cold water from the well, a tart red apple, a bird on a telephone wire.

For these lessons, dear Lord, I thank you.

For his great love for our mother, I thank you.

Because he thought her the most beautiful woman in the world, we did too. Because he worshiped her, courted her, waited on her, we too revered and adored her. And while this may have spoiled us (we thought all marriages were like theirs), it is a happy thing to remember.

For this, dear Lord, I thank you.

I am glad that of all the men you might have chosen, it was he who brought me into being. Thank you for this father, Lord.

Thank you for this man we call Dad!

A Woman's Name

Listen, Lord, please listen . . .

I miss myself sometimes. I even miss my name.

How is it, I wonder, that I have become just "Mother," "Mom," or "Honey"? Words that are tender and kindly but simply don't conjure up *me*. The person I really am.

I sometimes long for the sound of my whole given name. And my last name too. The name that first marked me as belonging to my parents, blood of their blood, name of their name.

You know how truly grateful I am to be a good man's wife. Entitled to stand before the world as *Mrs.* Glad that I bear my husband's name. A name of honor and achievement; and that I am proud that he is the summary and epitome of all the qualities of that name.

But isn't something vital lost when, even through marriage, anyone assumes another person's name? Isn't that the first subtle erosion of a woman's identity? To be known no longer as herself but as merely an adjunct to a man?

Cleave to each other, we are told. Become one flesh. And in most matters let the man be master.

I agree with this, Lord. I believe this is not only your will but good sense. However we may rail against it, seek to escape it, it is wise because it is natural. It works. It makes for a stronger home.

Yet how can a woman ever discover her own soul's value if she is nothing but echo and shadow of a man?

Lord, you know I love my husband and cherish the protection and even the status of his name. But don't let me forget who I am. Let me cling to myself, too.

Please don't let me ever lose the precious individuality you created, if only through the simple symbol of my name.

Mother And Son

Listen, Lord, please listen . . .

Can a woman ever really know her son?

Could even Mary understand Jesus? His passions, his needs, his secret drives? Did she ever stand as I do at the door of her boy's room, feeling helpless? Her love flowing out to him in a terrible tide that only washes back upon itself because it can lightly touch and comfort, but never truly penetrate and sustain.

Is the mind of any woman, even a mother, equipped to cope with the mystery of any man?

My son talks to me often—freely, excessively almost, and yet the mystery remains. I cannot follow his logic, accept his conclusions. And however gently or vigorously I try to reason, he strikes my reasoning aside.

Again he goes his own way in silence—often a silence so obviously born of suffering that I am wild to share it and perhaps assuage. But grim experience has taught me to leave him alone.

I am almost beside myself sometimes, God. Why should he elude me, this young stranger whom I brought into being? For he needs me, too. He turns to me, often when it is outrageously inconvenient, demanding that I rescue him from this plight or that, give him my energy, time, advice.

And I yield because I love him; we are briefly close.

Lord, what is this emotional tug-of-war between mother and son?

As I lay it before you I begin to see how almost comically hopeless it is. It is simply—life.

No. The answer is—no. No woman can ever truly know her son.

Emotionally and biologically he is different. The mere fact that my body shaped and delivered this male creature does not make us in the slightest way the same.

The best I can do is thank you for him and keep on loving him and bumble along as best I can. Knowing that I can't spare him pain, or hope to penetrate the secret chambers of his being. But that in silence or in fervent conversation I *am* helping him by simply being here, someone on whom he can depend.

And this is quite a lot. Thank you, Lord, for showing me that this is really quite a lot.

Must We Dominate Each Other?

Lord, deliver us from all this jockeying for position in marriage. This pulling and tugging for domination.

Now my husband seems to have the advantage and I am subservient, striving to please—and appease. Or I am the one who has things going my way, while he is docile and humble, to my vague delight and disdain.

We both sense that there is something awfully wrong with this picture, but we seem powerless to change it. Our natures seem locked in some subtle combat. Even as we deplore it, we find ourselves acting out these daily patterns of "Now it's your turn, now it's mine."

You, who joined us in this partnership, deliver us from its destructive divisiveness. Help us to stop trying to get ahead of each other, so that together we can get ahead with the important things.

Lord, help us to build each other up, to become the best possible team. One, not only in body but in spirit.

Our love is strong enough to do it. Your love is strong enough to help us do it. Thank you for that help, Lord.

The Divorcee

Lord, my friend is having a hard time adjusting since her divorce.

"Who am I?" she used to cry, bewailing her restrictions. The seeming waste of herself as merely the wife of a successful man, the mother of his children. She felt she had to assert herself, do something else, break free.

But now that she's free, she's bewildered.

The children have been divided up and put away in schools. She's no longer suffocating in the role of Mother. She's not even a successful man's wife anymore.

She's nobody. At least right now. The self she expected to discover simply didn't appear.

And the children, Lord. They too are confused.

The dividing up of lives has been a shock to them. They haven't a whole family to identify with anymore. They too are asking, more frantically than she did: "Who am I? Where do I belong?"

And the father—his own image of himself has been shattered. He too is struggling to find some meaning and value to his life, now that his accustomed role is gone.

Lord, help them all. The father, the mother, the children.

Speak to them in their loneliness, guide them to other people who will help give them back a sense of identity.

Above all, let them realize how important they still are to you. That they will always belong to you.

How Important Is Sex?

Oh, God, in this wonderful scheme of man in relation to woman, and woman to man, help me to understand the true significance of sex:

How important it is in coming fully to know someone we love. How vital to human communion. The rich fulfillment, the total commitment. This I think I understand.

But why is it so many men think only in terms of superficial sex?

That they can't accept a friendship, a good sound stimulating meeting of minds without thinking it must also lead to bed?

Did you create woman so vulnerable or so seductive that men instinctively consider this her only role of consequence?

Or man so predominately the powerful animal that he expects woman to see him primarily in this light?

Not all men, no.

I shall always be grateful to you for the wonderful friendships I have enjoyed with good, wise, inspiring, genuine, helpful, non-sex-preoccupied men.

Yet there are so many of the other kind. Help me to understand their motives better—their vanity perhaps, their insecurity, their pride.

And help me to conduct myself with them so that they won't misunderstand mine.

The Priceless Gift

Lord of life, creator of man and woman, thank you for the priceless gift of sex. Sex as you intended it long ago in the garden at time's beginning, when they saw that they were naked. Innocent, without responsibility, they hadn't realized. But in their hard-won wisdom they saw, and covered themselves.

I don't think it was their shame, God. It was the instinct you gave them, their basic common sense. For the marvel of their differentness was enhanced by the shielding leaves.

They achieved mystery for each other; they achieved a sweet excitement and new worth. And they achieved another very precious thing—personal privacy. The right to keep to oneself the most important part of oneself.

In this way I think you conveyed to man and woman the true wonder and beauty of sex. Secret not because of being shameful but because of its infinite value. Something too significant in the scheme of human happiness to be lightly exposed.

Lord of life, creator of man and woman, thank you for the joyous fulfillment of sex. When this marvelous secret is shared between two people who deeply love each other. Shared freely, generously, completely, without shame.

Thank you for this most perfect of all human delights, most profound of all human communions. This that regenerates both body and spirit.

The most vital act of life, the very core and source

of life. Help us to appreciate and revere it always, the priceless gift of sex.

Don't Let Me Compete With Men

Hear me, dear Lord . . .

However ambitious I may be, don't let me compete with men.

I want to succeed, yes—but, oh God, don't let success ever become more significant than my own sexuality.

You made me first and foremost a woman. Even though I enter fields traditionally associated with men, let me work there *as* a woman. Bringing a woman's insight, a woman's special gifts.

Let men think of me as a woman, respect and love me as a woman.

Let me remember always that you made men and women to complement each other. To enhance the values of each other, not to lock horns and struggle for supremacy.

Don't let my achievements, whatever they may be, make me the enemy of any man. Don't let money ever become more important to me than the companionship and affection, the cherishing of a man.

Keep me always a womanly woman. A man's kind of woman. Don't let me compete with men.

Woman and the World

So I returned, and considered all the oppressions that are done under the sun: and behold the tears of such as were oppressed.

ECCLESIASTES 4:1

I Wish I Didn't Feel
So Guilty

I wish I didn't feel so guilty, God.
Tried and found guilty of sins I didn't commit.
Drugs. Violence. Crime. Racism. Poverty. War.
They assault me from all sides. I cringe from the constant sight and sound of them. I want to run and hide, to bury my head, saying, "No, no, let me alone, I have not brought this about."

I don't want to march. I don't want to join protests.
I feel my place is not in the picket line but behind the picket fence. Yet even the little domain behind that fence is threatened. My home is threatened, my children's school is threatened. My children's very lives are threatened.

And here I stand helpless, saying, "Go away crime and war and violence and drugs and prejudice. I didn't spawn you, I don't practice you, I hate and detest you, but I'm too busy to fight you. Don't drag me out of my safe little place that I have worked so hard to establish. I haven't the time, I haven't the energy, I haven't the will."

Yet I am gnawed by the guilt of my own seeming cowardice and selfishness. A sense of some dark and criminal omission.
Lord, is this false or is it real? Will I really be helping or changing anything by putting down my daily tasks and charging forth into these battles?
Please show me my true priorities—as a parent and

as a responsible Christian. Please give me guidance, God.

The Nursery

There they lie, in their little glass garden, these fragile new fruits of human love. And of your love too, the eternal love that flows through the universe, creating and re-creating these exquisite creatures in your image.

There they sleep, God, in the blessed sleep of their newness. So fresh from the mystery of their beginning, so warm and moist and sweet from the waters in which they were cradled.

Resting from the rude shock of birth they lie. . . . Resting . . . resting for the long journey ahead.

Though one or two awake and start yelling—lustily, comically demanding the rescue that quickly comes. Hands, gently efficient, to change and feed and comfort them. To hold them up before the pleased eyes of the people gazing in.

There they sleep, God, or are displayed, wrapped in the most complete and absolute love they will ever know.

Then one grandmother, old and broken with living, smiles faintly and shakes her head. "Poor little things," she remarks as she turns away. "If they only knew what's ahead."

And my heart gives a little start of sorrow. I too am suddenly stricken. For I see these children rising and walking, stripped of protection, of warm blankets and sheltering arms.

I see some of them cold, frightened, struggling—against danger, violence, physical abuse, drugs. I see them tempted, I see them shaken. I see them bitter with heartbreak, confusion, despair. And my whole being cries out to you, "No, no, spare them, keep them here!"

But I know you wouldn't have it so. *They* wouldn't have it. They are as hungry for the life struggle as they are for milk. It is their right; they are savagely insistent upon it.

They sleep now ... However sweetly they sleep now ... they must rise up and go. But oh, Lord, when the blissful sleep is over and they take their first faltering steps, give us patience, give us wisdom. Show us how to help them.

For now, bless them as they lie resting for the journey ahead.

Forgive Them

Father, forgive all the people who are using their God-given talents to profit from sex corruption. Forgive them for the damage they are doing to our children. Forgive them for the big lie they are selling to the world.

Forgive them for the scared kids who find themselves in trouble, deep trouble, and don't know where to turn. Forgive them for the distraught parents, the hours of family agony.

Forgive them for the deaths they have caused on abortionists' tables. For the homes they fill with unmarried mothers. For the Gethsemane of even one little girl being wheeled, alone, frightened and friendless, to a delivery room.

Forgive them for the guilt-ridden boys who know they have fathered children they will never see. Forgive them for the bewildered, disillusioned youngsters forced into marriage too soon.

Father, forgive them for the broken hearts and broken homes. For the husbands and wives they have helped to "liberate," only to discover that adultery, however alluring, demands its pound of flesh in return.

Forgive them for the divorces they have directly contributed to. And for the children of these tragedies whom they have helped to torment and to rob.

Father, forgive the pictures—written, painted or enacted—that so artfully seduce. That make sex so enticing and so free, and lust and even aberration fascinating.

Forgive them the books, the movies and the plays. They have taken the most magical media of entertainment, escape and instruction we have ever known and turned them into one vast juggernaut to arouse our emotions, destroy our values and crush our disciplines and decencies.

And they have done this for one reason: Because it sells.

Father, forgive them. Not because "they know not what they do." They do know. And they don't care.

But what profit a man if he loses his own soul and takes the souls of others with him?

Father, save us from this prostitution of your gifts. Father, forgive them.

For A Little Lost Family

He's so young and lost and ill-equipped for life, Lord, help him, help him.

His neck is still thin and unformed. His shoulders are so narrow, too narrow for the manly burdens he's assumed. His mind isn't ready for these responsibilities yet either, and neither is his nature.

He shouldn't be tied to this little-girl wife, going home to bills and babies. He should be in school. He should be preparing himself for the mighty job of being a man—a husband, a father, instead of being plunged into the middle of it.

He's bewildered, Lord. He's groping. He's trying to act out a role he's not ready for. And his wife is so young and bewildered and lonely and unready too.

They were neither of them ready for marriage. They were just playing house, and now, appallingly, it's real. They are both tired of it already.

What will become of them, God? What will become of their beautiful baby?

Please, God, help these three children. Help this little lost family.

Miracle On The Moon

Here we are, God, sitting in our quiet houses watching man set foot carefully, oh so carefully, upon the moon.

Awe and wonder grip us. How can this be? we ask, in an agony of reverent suspense. How does man dare to leave this planet on which you have placed him, and blast off into space to claim the moon?

What manner of brave bright effrontery is this that he sets himself down carefully, however carefully, upon its mysterious alien substance and stands at last erect upon the moon?

It is surely to witness a miracle. It is like being present on one of the first days when you created the earth and the heavens and this bold incredible creature, man himself.

We huddle like children on the sidelines. Like souls yet unborn. We are almost speechless with excitement; our very admiration and amazement make us dumb.

We can only thank you, God, for bringing these men safely to their incredible destination. And for the miracle of being able to watch it from the earth, in our safe, comfortable homes.

We know that the age of miracles is not over. You continue to perform your miracles—little ones in our lives every day, and great ones like this. When even the heavens are subject to man's genius, under your direction. When you guide man, your dear creation, safely to the destination of his dreams upon the moon.

The Battered Child

I'm glad I didn't play bridge today and stuff myself. I'm glad I didn't go shopping and spend money for things I don't need. I'm glad I didn't stay at home, bemoaning my miseries.

Thank you with all my heart that I was led instead to that battered child.

She was so cruelly hurt, Lord. Thank you that I was there to hold her. To feel that little body that shook so terribly at first go quiet against the warmth of mine. To see those huge fright-dazed eyes change into something resembling the eyes of a child.

Thank you that I was there to wipe her tears and blow her nose and rock her. That she actually laughed a little over the pictures and the stories. That she was still clinging to me when she finally curled up and went to sleep. And that when she wakes up there will be others to hold and comfort her.

Oh God, dear God, forgive and heal and help the people who misuse little children. And somehow, in your wisdom and mercy, spare and rescue those children.

Make the courts realize that they must not be returned to people who only damage helpless children.

This evil is so stark, so insane, it is more than the rest of us can comprehend. Please give us the power to prevent it. And until then the courage and the energy at least to comfort and try to heal and help the tiny victims.

Thank you for leading me to that little girl.

This Crisis Of Birth Control

Oh, God, have mercy upon all the women for whom physical love results in unwanted conceptions.

Bless them in their dismay, anguish, despair. Give them understanding, give them answers.

Surely you did not mean this fiercely beautiful attraction of the human sexes to be limited to procreation.

You did not make us beasts of the fields; we do not mate only at certain seasons to replenish our kind. We meet and mate to replenish ourselves—our joy, our peace, our sense of union.

This was your plan. This, surely, your vital plan for us.

Yet, forgive me—something is wrong with this plan if it only means more babies than we can feed or clothe or shelter or properly send to school. If it results in heartbreak, shame or hardships to children already here.

If it actually begins to threaten human survival.

How can an instinct so intense, so insistent and sweet, be right if its results are these? How can it even be fair?

God, help each of us to find the answer in accordance with your will for us.

In reverence and sincerity we ask for ways to bring

into this world only those lives that have a fair chance
to be whole lives.

God, our creator, all wise and all seeing, see our
plight and give us wisdom to deal with this crisis that
comes from physical love.

Charity Ward

Dear God, please help these people in the charity
ward.

They are suffering, they are sick, they are scared.
Too scared or stupefied, some of them, even to ask for
help or do what they could to help themselves.

They sit stolidly awaiting their turns—for treatment
or for death. The blind film of a desperation beyond
desperation is on their eyes.

They come without hope, many of them; they come
out of some dumb, instinctive habit. And the staff are
too overworked and underpaid or dulled by this same
overexposure to suffering to give what the poor people really want most—genuine interest in their problems, genuine caring. Some of these people are cyni-
cal, Lord, some even cruel.

Thank God for those doctors and nurses and aides
who do seem to care, who are wonderfully patient
and kind. But their number is limited, and so is their
strength and their time.

Work a miracle, Lord. Multiply their number, extend their compassion, deepen and widen their reser-
voirs of sympathy, skill and strength.

And oh, Father, help these hordes who come because there is no place else to go.

They are your children too, my brothers and sisters in want. Deliver them from despair, and the rest of us from indifference.

Help them—and help me to know how to help them.

Black Is Beautiful

They say black is beautiful, Lord, and I agree.

Black is beautiful, like the rich black earth of the Middle West where I was born. Beautiful like the velvet darkness of the night.

If I were an artist I would choose to paint black faces. The structure of many black faces, their expression of nobility, sorrow or exuberance, is very beautiful to me.

Black arms cradled my white babies; black hands have scrubbed my floors. Black teachers have taught me, black artists have thrilled me, the achievements of great black people have been an inspiration for me. I have laughed and wept with my black brothers and sisters, and they have laughed and wept with me.

But you are not color-blind, God. You saw quite well what you were doing in creating black people and white people and people whose skins are other hues. We are all your children, and surely equally dear to you.

That we have enslaved each other, hurt each other, is an affront to our creator. But oh God, please don't punish us for the sins of our forefathers.

Let us acknowledge those awful wrongs. Let us continue to do our best to right them. But those of us who have always known the beauty of black people, those who have honestly tried, don't feel that we deserve black hate.

Hate is never beautiful. White hate. Or black hate.
Hate is ugliness. Only love is beautiful.

Please let your love for all of us flood us now. So
that we can truly find beauty in each other and come
together in love to resolve our differences.

Women And War

What is a woman to do about war?

Isn't it enough that war must rage in the human
spirit? Or that we must forever do battle with dirt
and confusion and the conflicts within a family? Or
fight the eternal hopeless battle against growing old?

Why must there be this other war as well, Lord?

Husbands torn away from us for months, years,
sometimes never to come back at all. Or returned to
us broken in body and soul, blinded, dismembered,
scarred beyond scarring, wounded in ways that we
can't even know.

And our sons, mere boys led into the senseless
slaughter. Our children, to whom we taught compassion, now taught to be savages to survive. This non-
sense of lives interrupted and ruined, Lord. This
whole bloody butchery of war.

I shake my fist in your face sometimes and demand
that you stop it. Or I fall prostrate and beg, "Please!"
Yet the insanity goes on, each time with an intensity
unmatched before.

In the name of Christ, who was supposed to bring
peace, where is that peace now?

Yet I know that we dare not demand peace as a
gift to be wrung from your pity and your power. We
were once shown the ways to peace, and those ways
were hard but clear. Very clear.

If man refuses to heed, then war is no fault of yours. So long as there is evil in the world and war in men's hearts, there will be war.

Thank you for this grim knowledge, Lord. I must continue to trust you. Surely more than ever in times of war.

My Country

Please heal and comfort and restore my beautiful battered country.

Let its waters flow clean again, God. Show us how to cleanse them.

Let its air be fit to breathe again, God. Give us ways, give us wisdom.

Let its poor gouged sides grow green again. Nourish its soil, which we have starved or ruined in our greed. Arrest its cancerous tumors and blights of wastes and slums.

I pray this for the breath and body of America, Lord. I pray for its physical healing.

But I pray even more for its spirit.

Its character, God, that once stood strong as its forests, brisk and sure and sparkling as its waters. That too has been muddied by filth, wounded, debased, torn asunder. So that it reels before the world, bewildered, asking, "Who am I?" and fears to hear the answers.

My country, God—my decent, generous country that has sacrificed for others, poured out tides of

blood and money—that it should come to this. Casti-
gated. Hated. No, no, I won't have it!

Oh, God, give America back the strength it had as
a young new nation, knowing who it was and crying
its name with pride.

God, I pray for its very survival. My great and
beautiful country that has given more freedom and a
better life to more people than any other nation since
the world began. Defend us from its attackers. Stay
the hand of those who would destroy it.

Open their eyes to its wonders. Let them bear
witness to its progress as well as its faults. Turn their
energies to the task of building instead of burning.

Oh, God, don't let them take it away. Don't let
them bring it down to destruction.

Surely you love America, God, or you wouldn't
have endowed it so richly.

We are sorry for our failures; we repent, we are
trying desperately to make amends. Please forgive us
all that is past and help us.

Oh, God, please heal and restore my beloved country.

The Woman Aware

Truly the light is sweet, and a pleasant thing it is for the eyes to behold the sun.

ECCLESIASTES 11:7

Five Senses

You have given me five senses, God.

Five keen instruments for knowing and savoring your wonderful world.

Without sight I would walk in darkness.

Without hearing, in silence.

Without taste and smell I would miss the myriad flavors that enhance and heighten living.

Without touch I would be as something wooden, I would never know the feeling of flesh against my own, or the texture of all the things that tell us, "Yes, you are real, you exist, you are here."

With my mind I think. With my emotions I react. With my spirit and whole being I worship and love.

But almost everything that reaches my inner being must first come to me through these marvelous instruments of awareness.

Thank you, God, for these five senses which give me contact with all the things and beings in your beautiful world.

The Jewels

Thank you, Lord, for the priceless jewels you have given me.

I look up at night, and the skies are riddled with

sapphires. I wake up in the morning, and my clothesline is strung with pearls.

It rains, and when the rain is over, gold streams across my backyard, scattering a riot of gems.

It snows, and my front steps are dusted with diamonds. Another diamond clings for an hour to a bush in the sun, sparkling like the Star of Africa.

I have a great fire opal. Night after night it lifts its burning face to me and slowly parades for my pleasure, replenishing itself and glowing with more intensity as the weeks pass. Then with each new month I am given a new one to admire.

No thieves can rob me of them, God. They can never be lost, they require no insurance.

And I need feel no guilt at having such fabulous treasures in the face of hungry people, people in want. For they too own every shining gem in the universe.

It takes only the heart to reach out to them, the eyes to claim them.

Thank you for the priceless jewels you have given all of us.

"And God Saw That It Was Good"

With you there need be no ugliness, God. Not when we see with the eyes of you who made the world, and saw that it was good. For you created no ugliness. And you have given us the power to find beauty in even the drab, the unsightly, the man-made ugliness.

A hospital, a slum, a littered city street, a backyard

where dirty snow is melting ... There is beauty and wonder even here when the eyes are bright for living and the heart is filled with love. The greatest artists have painted humble, even ugly things.

Van Gogh awoke to the raw beauty of the poverty-stricken miners when he was carrying your message to the Belgian Borinage. From their care-wracked faces bending gratefully over a meal came "The Potato Eaters." Toulouse-Lautrec found beauty among the brothels; Grant Wood in a chicken house, a field of corn.

We are not all artists, God. But our eyes can shape our own masterpieces, whatever the landscape of our lives, wherever we look.

Thank you, though it tore me at the time, for a wonderful picture that will hang always on my heart—a tiny girl who'd found a pile of ashes and was heaping and patting and sifting it in lieu of sand. The silver cone of the ash pile, the delicate haze of its dust. And the enchantment on the grubby face as she squatted, absorbed, in the sun.

She had discovered her sand pile, her own shining seashore. In the innocence of childhood, she had taken the discard of the adult world and turned it into treasure.

Let me see all things in this world with the enthralled naked eyes of the artist, Lord. Or the pure wondering eyes of that child.

Let me find the beauty that lies in all the substance of living, in the grim as well as the good.

The Streetlamps

The river lies black and shining, coins of brightness blazing on its satin breast.

The wind strikes them, breaks and shatters them into little snakes and scribbles of gold, silver, scarlet. Then they fall into place once more, coins and sequins, scattered gems.

On the far bank the streetlights form a rhythmic, looping pattern against the darkness. The lamps stand at the apex, each in its misty tent. Each like a star at the crest of a lonely little steeple.

A star or an eye burning steadily through the night, mystical, serene, staving off the darkness, offering its little tented shelter of illumination.

I feel the finger of God in this glimpse of beauty.

I sense the linking of man's hand and God's in creating this bit of beauty in the night.

Spring Wind

Your spring wind, Lord, is a bullying boy.

It snatches the clothes I am trying to pin on the line and whips them about my face.

It grabs the lids of trash barrels and sends them spinning like silver hoops.

It yanks the vines like a little girl's braids.

It shakes the blossom-laden trees, and the sweet confetti of their petals rains down upon me.

Your white clouds rush headlong before it. Your great trees bow and sway. Your flowers bend to its caprice.

The wind is a rollicking peddler, crying his wonderful wares, browbeating the world to buy.

I love your spring wind, Lord.

Its bright prancing. It makes me want to dance too, to roll a hoop, throw confetti, gather armloads of flowers (instead of clothes).

Your vigor is in it. Your joy is in it. Your infinite lively artistry is in it.

Thank you for spring wind, Lord.

Make Me Aware Of People

Lord, make me aware of the wonder of people. All kinds of people, old or young, important or humble, neighbor or child or foreigner or stranger on the street.

You have made us all so marvelously varied. Outwardly so different in face and form and circumstance, yet basically so much alike. Each of us going his own way with such private passion, locked in his tiny universe of self. However we strive to share, give, communicate, we are bounded by the limited horizons of our own concerns.

God, make me more vitally cognizant of these other worlds spinning behind all these faces. Such complex, fascinating worlds, filled with memories, worries, anxieties, philosophies, ambitions, experiences.

Remind me to listen, really listen when people open their mouths, like small doors to that world, and try to share what's inside. Remind me to look, really look, into the hopeful windows of their eyes. I can never really enter, no, but how much I can learn from these brief glimpses. How much my own world can be expanded. (And how much I can give just by listening.)

Help me not to go coasting off on the barge of my own conceits, or wait in half-deaf exasperation for my turn. Help me to realize the marvel of being invited even to the doorstep of another person's world.

Lord, make me always aware of the wonder of people.

People who live and think and breathe and feel, the same as I do. People laughing, crying, loving, hurting, touching.

People gazing into store windows ... hailing taxis ... scrubbing floors. People holding warm new babies ... smelling the flowers in a funeral chapel. People with the sand hot against their feet on a windy beach ... or a cold sidewalk bitter through broken shoes.

The sheer wonder of people, God. In joy or torment or the little acts of every day. Your people. My people. An extension of you, and so of each of us.

If I can identify with other people, taste their tears as well as mine, rejoice in their rejoicing, then I can be more completely your creation, and more aware of who I am myself.

The Quiet Hour

Listen, listen, Lord ...

Listen with me to this quiet hour of evening when the dishes are done and the family wanders about outside.

There are no meetings tonight, no committees, no dates, no rehearsals—just this quiet time when people are doing what they want. Thank you—and bless it:

My husband watering the grass. The musical sound of the water, the faint cool kiss of its spray. And the sweet lively scent of the good green earth quenching its thirst.

A daughter sprawled on a lawn swing, reading. A son on the back steps, untangling a fishing reel. Two little boys quarreling over a coaster wagon ... Bless them all, and give me the good sense not to interfere, even with the fight.

I am tired. I will claim this old blanket left over from a doll picnic this afternoon. I will stretch out on its hummocky surface and gaze up into your evening sky, where the light still lingers.

There is a long blue opening, framed in a ragged outline by the branches of trees. And in this open space birds sail, wings twinkling, and bats dip swift as jets. While all about is the twittering of sleepier birds, and the nodding, murmuring leaves.

As I lie here, listening, the leaves are revealed in their remarkable individuality. Their dozen different, cleanly printed shapes.

Some round, yet tapering like fingers at the tips. Some like stars. Some like flat, many-fingered hands.

I note too in sharp silhouette this way the pattern of their growing upon the branches, the exquisite rhythms of their designs. The delicate form and fitting of their twigs. And my heart is filled with wonder at your works.

The leaves bow and murmur as if in agreement with my thoughts: This is the best hour of the day.

This is contentment. This is God.

White Wings

The whole sky tonight has become a great milk-white bird, poised on the edge of the horizon, wings outspread.

White, white, layered and feathered with clouds, they stretch the heavens wide, these wings.

Between them, padded and layered and feathered deep is the body of a swan, its white breast arched. And through a hole in its center, plucked bare and pure and clean, the moon shines through like a round white burning heart.

It is like glimpsing the gentle glowing of your own heart, God.

Psalm For Autumn

I draw back the draperies in the morning and my eyes are filled with the glory of the Lord. I cross my own backyard or drive along the roadside, and my senses are almost overcome.

He has lavished his beauty upon us, he has painted the earth for our delight. His colors are more than the eye can contain. They take on other dimensions, they cry and shimmer and shout, they crackle and sail about; like the birds, they sing.

These gleaming yellow torches of poplars and beeches and elms. The winy purple of these Japanese maples; and the brilliant sunset shades of the other maples nearby.

And the crimson fringe of the sumac, like the fringe of a gypsy's shawl. And the nameless little orange vines that zigzag like spurts of fire up the silvery trunks of trees.

While all this is laced and spattered and interwoven with the shimmering blue of the sky and the radiant remaining green.

How am I worthy of such wonder? How is it that I, small and human and faulty, can witness this magnificence along with saints and kings?

I don't know. I only know that each autumn this fiery baptism draws me closer to my creator.

The Snow

Frail stars are falling as I look out the window, Lord. Tiny sparks that catch the sun. Bits of sparkling fluff that kiss the earth, then vanish, though some of them settle and cling.

Inside, a fire gossips on the grate. Like a contented grandmother the teakettle clucks and sings.

The coffee is hot and fragrant as I serve it to my
friends. And my heart is full ... the coziness, the
companionship ... So precious, so quickly over.

For now the friends are leaving, calling good-byes.
Their feet leave small black prints on the walk's white
dusting. But even this evidence of their presence is
swiftly covered and gone.

Softly, silently, the snow continues to fall. Into the
evening, into the night. Twining down like Maypole
ribbons yet still glittering in the light of passing cars.

The errant stars are caught in the delicate stream-
ers. They sparkle in the hair of the silent unseen
dancers, winding their ribbons. Graceful, fleet-footed,
the invisible dancers wind the world, muffling and
binding it as if in some ancient secret rite.

Now it is morning, God, and the world lies still.
Robed in splendor. Shining, shining before the first
stroking and touching and testing of the sun. Yester-
day's naked trees are wrapped in a white effulgence,
each branch a clutch of treasure, shedding glittering
veils when the wind stirs.

And the sun in dazzling command. The sun
drawing fiery lines along those bowed branches and
slender trunks. Turning them into strips of shadow
across the uncluttered white expanse, or lacy patterns
impossible before.

The sun, at once the enhancer and eventual
claimer of all this loveliness.

Lord—the sweet, eternal mystery of snow.

The tiny sparks falling with such uncertainty upon
bare earth and the simple human scene. Then mount-
ing to such awesome, brilliant immensity ... only to
be tracked, shoveled, enjoyed, deplored, cursed ...
and melt away.

Are we too like the snow? So frail at first, our time upon this earth so bright, so brief. It is over so quickly. The fire on the grate ... the coffee in the hand ... the friends who come and go ...

And the snow, the beautiful mystery of the snow.

God, let me savor every instant of life while it lasts. Before I too vanish into the glorious sun of your presence, like the snow.

All Your Living Creatures

Lord, thank you for the miracle of all other creatures. Make me always aware of their special nature and purpose, and their needs.

The dog at my knee, the cat warm on my shoulder, the birds whose brisk chiming so joyfully herald my day. The moths at my window at night, Lord ... yes, even the ants that sometimes invade my kitchen.

Comfort, companion, beauty or nuisance, let me marvel at their existence; remembering that whether large as an elephant or smaller than the smallest snail, within each is a system of cells and circulation quite as complex and ingenious as that you gave to me. That within each body beats a heart as hungry for life as my own.

Let me respect that life force, Lord, and destroy nothing needlessly. And let me be merciful when I do.

If I must catch fish (and I like to, though I'm not much good at it), let me end its gasping quickly. If I must eat meat (and it can't be wrong, since you provided so many animals mainly for our nourishment), let me do all in my power to see that those who kill for my table do so mercifully.

If helpless animals must be sacrificed to minimize human suffering and extend the life of man, it is my duty in common decency to make sure that their suffering is minimized as well.

Dumb, unable to speak for themselves, except for pleading eyes or sometimes eloquent tails, they beg our compassion, they beg our love and care and understanding.

Lord, don't let me ever stand idly by or turn my eyes away from any cruelty or injustice to any of your creatures.

Help me to defend them, cherish and enjoy them, without losing sight of the fact that you made them—fish and birds and animals—for the service and comfort of man.

As such, they are a sacred responsibility. As someone has said, "A link between man and God's silent, unseen self." Thank you for this mysterious link, for it is both a test and a tribute to our faithfulness.

Sight On A Moonlit Road

The leaves are still frail and new, a tremulous green dusting upon these tall old trees. And just below them the dogwoods are a delicate white mist of bloom. Only a red suggestion of buds a few days ago, now the flat, faintly cupped petals are upheld, like some display of precious china in a jeweler's window.

The moon enhances their translucent purity. The very roadway, dark by day, is white with its flooding.

The black and white dog bounding along ahead has a luminous quality. And the cat, which has slipped out and pats silently behind, is also shining. White face and paws echo the Dalmatian's spotted body in tinier dots that weave through the shadows. Like little floating stars or petals in the fragrant chirping night.

A utility pole beside the road is illuminated too, its black spear and crossbar moon-rimmed. Turning, I see its startling shadow lying across the moon-white road.

A cross! A leaning cross, moon-etched. Tender, graceful, and not really sad. Only poignant. A poignant reminder of suffering. The Lord's suffering and triumph. All human suffering and triumph.

A moving sight on a moonlit roadway.

The Adventure

Oh, God, I rejoice in the sheer adventure of living.

Just to wake up in the morning and face the bright mystery of the day!

Even though I think I know, I can't possibly know what will happen before it's over. How many times will the telephone ring, bringing me what voices? What news will come in the mail?

Whom will I meet? Whom will I see? What good friend, what exciting stranger? And no matter how familiar the people who share my hours, what will they do or say?

All these people in the wings of my life waiting to make their entrances. Waiting to speak their lines, to

engage me in dialogue that will affect each of us in so
many ways.

Words of love, anger, argument, merriment, persua-
sion, praise—an infinite variety of lines unwritten,
unrehearsed, full of pain or promise, or the simple
small exchanges of everyday.

How wonderful this is, God. How endlessly in-
triguing this daily drama of living.

Now a comedy, now a tragedy, but always, always
full of expectation. Always a mystery!

It's Been A Good Day

It's been a good day, Lord. Yes, a very good day.

I didn't realize it while it was happening. There
were many frustrations. I was very discouraged when
the letter I was praying for didn't come. Then the
telephone rang, bringing good news.

When a child was carried home from the playground hurt and we rushed him to the hospital, you
knew my awful fears. But to learn that it wasn't really
serious brought a sense of heightened joy. (Sheer
relief can generate sheer bliss.)

So now the child is asleep, with the bandage
slipped rather comically from his head. My husband
stands in the yard, leaning on his rake as he visits with
a neighbor.

Other children come spilling across the yard. The
sun is a golden glory behind the trees. I can smell the
pot roast mingling with the tangy fragrance of burning leaves.

I look back on this day with its usual ups and
downs. Its moments of anguish, its moments of grate-

fulness and joy. And now that it's ending, an aching awareness fills me. I realize that it's been a good day, Lord. A very good day.

For it's been filled with life. The life you have given me to cope with, and to contribute to. And I wouldn't want to have missed it, not a single moment of it.

Thank you, God, for this good day.

I Shall Go To Sleep

I shall go to sleep. . . . I shall go to sleep.

In the blessed peace of your presence I shall go to sleep.

I shall lie down in my bed as in your green pastures.

I shall stretch out and drift off as beside your still waters.

And as I sleep, my cup of cares will vanish, my joys will return and run over. As I drink deep of your rest I know you will be restoring my soul.

My dreams will be filled with your blessings; my strength will be replenished. I shall wake in the morning renewed in body and spirit, ready for the work you have given me, the life you have willed me to live. Knowing your goodness and mercy will fill me all the days that are ahead.

For now, oh God, I shall simply thank you and go to sleep.

The Good Night's Sleep

Thank you, God, for that good night's sleep.

My body is all soft and relaxed and yet so refreshed.

No ache nor pain disturbed my rest. No voice summoned me, no noise disturbed me.

I not only drifted off into sweet oblivion, but wandered in the mysterious mists of dreams. And these dreams were gay and tender and filled with a gentle excitement.

I danced, flew, floated. Romped with a long-lost pet. Saw people dear to me, people I'll never see again in life—my parents, an old sweetheart. We laughed and talked and touched.

And though the memories of these dreams are vanishing swiftly, their radiance remains.

Thank you, God, for putting sleep into the scheme of us.

This marvelous escape from the trials of the day. This beautiful way to refurbish our strength for the tasks of tomorrow.

Perhaps sleep, good sleep, is a little sample of one ultimate tomorrow. Where we will have no need of bodies. Where we will find perfect reunion with people we love.

Perhaps sleep, even one good night's sleep, is a preview of eternity.

Woman on the Move

And I will send an angel before thee.   EXODUS 33:2

Trips

I think of all these trips, God.

Trips to the store, trips to the city, trips to a lake in the country. Little walking trips with the children or the dog.

Trips by car or bus or plane. Short trips, long trips, across the face of this fantastically varied world that you have made.

And I think how wonderful is this ability to move about. You have not deemed that your creatures stay in one place only; you have given us locomotion. Legs to walk with, arms to swim with, and all the different vehicles to ride in—so many ways to get about.

And my heart is filled with a sudden marveling joy.

How you must love us that you didn't lock us up in shells or caves. We can climb mountains, we can cross seas. We can shoot through the depths of your earth in tunnels; we can survey it from the skies.

Thank you for all this. That you who planted in us restlessness, the yearning to travel, gave us so many ways to gratify that need!

Big trips, little trips. Thank you for all of them, God. And be with us wherever we go.

The Welcome Move

Thank you, God, for the news of this move.

For the better job it means for my husband. For the new opportunities for us all.

Bless the people we are leaving behind. Please let them remember us kindly, and don't let us ever really lose those who have been so dear to us.

And bless the people we will meet in the place where we are going. I am excited when I think of them, Lord—strangers now, who will become a significant part of our lives.

Thank you for this mystery, this sense of anticipation. And guide us to the right ones, please. People whom we'll love and enjoy and whose lives will be enriched because of us.

Bless My Husband

Dear Lord, please bless my husband in this move.

Keep him as cheerful and enthusiastic as he is now.

Keep his vision bright. And give him time and strength for the countless things he has to do.

Not only the things to be finished on the job he's leaving, but the many things he must do for us. Getting rid of this home and finding us a new one. The paper work alone, the financial arrangements.

My mind boggles to think of it. I can only thank you that he is so capable, so dependable. So willing to shoulder the responsibilities of transporting us—furniture, possessions, kids, cats, dogs—to our new location.

(If a man visualized all this in the beginning, I sometimes wonder if he'd have the courage to get married.)

All this, plus the tremendous responsibilities he faces on this new undertaking.

Bless him, Lord. Support him, sustain him, don't let him get too tired. And please let this change be right for him, fulfill his highest expectations.

Thank you for taking care of my husband, God.

We Are Moving Again, And I Don't Want To Go

We are moving again, God, and I don't want to go.
I am sick and tired of moving.

I resent the time that must be squandered in packing and unpacking. In house selling and house hunting.

I don't want the children to have to change schools anymore. I don't want to have to make new friends anymore. I don't want to have to explain myself anymore, or try to find myself (or even my way around) in a new setting.

The adventure of moving has palled, Lord.
Setting off for a new city I used to think, "Some-

where out there it lies waiting for us. There in its vastness stands the place that will become home to us. There, right now, laughing and talking, are the people who will become important to us."

But now, oh Lord, this same prospect fills me only with a sense of being lost. Wanderers, strangers, with no real home to go to. Not really belonging anywhere, to anyone.

I have a sudden shocked awareness of how Mary and Joseph must have felt that night when they faced the careless crowds of Bethlehem and were told to be on their way.

I want to be able to put my roots down. Deep, deep.

How can I ever find out who I am if, so much of my life, I don't even know *where* I am?

Oh, God, hang onto me once more as I face the chaos and confusion of moving.

Help me to realize that you will go with us again, you will be with us again. I can talk to you wherever I am; I have a friend I can never lose in you wherever I am.

God, sustain me as I face this move.

A Prayer For Packing

How I dread packing, Lord.

Each time, no matter how often I've done it, it seems too much I just can't face it, I don't even know where to begin.

I gaze around this house, bursting with so many belongings, feeling only frustration and resistance. It took so long to get settled, and now this—to have to tear it all up again.

To go through the whole business of decisions— what to save, what to throw out, what to give away.

"I can't, I won't," a part of me protests.

These closets crammed with clothes. These cupboards filled with more dishes, vases, bric-a-brac than any of us ever use. These groaning shelves of books. These pictures, lamps, rugs.

Helplessly I regard them, yet with a kind of shamed new awareness. This proof of your generosity, God. This material abundance.

What kind of ingrate am I? And why have I held onto so much so long? When other people are cold and in want, what right have I to burden myself, and my own conscience, with this excess?

Instead of wringing my hands in despair, I ought to be rejoicing. I ought to be thanking you (and I am, right now).

Practically, I ought to be getting *started*. And with enthusiasm before the opportunity. To strip, to clean, to rid ourselves of the surplus baggage of living. To feel a fresh appreciation for the things we really care about. Above all, to realize how richly blessed we are to be able to share.

Thank you, God, for packing.

The Farewell Party

Thank you, God, for all these people who have gathered to tell us good-bye.

The ones we've been so close to and the ones we've rarely seen. The ones we've liked so much and even the ones who've been sometimes hard to take.

Now, curiously, they are all dear to us as we come together for the farewell party. Now suddenly I see who they are in relation to us—and who we must be in relation to them.

They are the living embodiment of time and place—our time in this particular place. They are themselves, yes, but in large or small ways they are changed because we came together. And we are changed because of them. We have interrelated; the precious stuff of our lives has touched.

What a miracle this is, what a blessing. That you created us, not to live alone or behind closed doors, but to brush against and help to color other lives.

And when this time is over, the parting hurts.

Friends taken for granted become strangely precious when it is time to separate.

Perhaps this is why these partings must come. To make us aware of each other, to realize our identities as characters in each other's life stories. To give us a little glimpse of who we are in the eyes of those who are our friends.

A farewell party—what a joy, however it hurts. What an honor. They love us enough to wish us well. "Fare well wherever you go," they are saying.

And we can only answer in kind, "Good-bye. Fare ... well."

Thank you for all these dear people, Lord. And bring us together again in another place, another time.

On Leaving A House

Oh, God, please bless this house that we are leaving.

We worked so hard to achieve it, put so much of ourselves into it, and now we must abandon it, and my heart aches foolishly.

I wander about the yard, noting the shrubs and bushes we set out. The peach tree should bloom and bear this year and we won't be here to see it! Forgive me for this sense of loss. Bless it. May it bear abundantly for the next people who live here.

And the patio. Our hands raked the sand, laid the bricks. Our feet, the feet of our family and our friends, walked them; we enjoyed so many cookouts and happy times here.

God, thank you for those times and may the smoke curl just as fragrantly and the food be just as good for those next ones.

This kitchen, Lord, almost but never quite the way I wanted. But my husband was so good to do so much. Thank you for his efforts, and the countless meals I cooked here.

For these gay little curtains I made and must take down. For the oven I am scrubbing so ardently for my successor. For all the casseroles it produced, the birthday cakes and holiday turkeys.

Bless the woman who will work here in my place. May this kitchen be her cozy shelter and the center of her activity. And may *she* have it just the way she wants.

God bless this fireplace, these bookshelves, this staircase. All these rooms, torn up now, rawly echoing to the tramp of movers' feet. Yet still throbbing with the life that sang and banged and burst within them. Our laughter, our quarrels and confusions. Our happiness and our agonies.

I can't bear it. I think for a minute I can't bear it—to leave this house for strangers, no matter what happened here.

It is a part of my life, Lord. My breath, my blood, my being. Cursing its defects, loving its comforts—my life and the life of my family was here.

Now you take my hand and lead me gently from this house.

A part of me is briskly directing the activity of moving, a part secretly crying, a part of me at peace.

"Good-bye, dear house," I can say. "Be a good house for them."

And thank you, God, for the part of my life that will always be here.

The New Home

Thank you that we are standing at last on the doorstep of our new home. Thank you that the long search is over; thank you for leading us to this place.

Bless this yard that will be our yard, and this street that will be our street.

May the yard be fruitful and green. May these

houses, filled with the people who will be our neighbors, become familiar and dear to us because of them.

May precious new bonds of human contact be formed because of this new home.

Bless this door that we are unlocking, Lord. And all the doors inside. Bless these rooms.

I move about them with gratefulness, sniffing their exciting smell of plaster and wood and bricks and paint. I examine their enticing strangeness.

Now, before we move in, tracking, yelling, hauling our possessions about—flood them with love and joy and peace.

I confirm your presence here in this new home. I claim your power to make this a good place for us. A safe place, a place of growth and understanding. A happy place.

May we all keep very close to you here, and to each other.

And may everyone on earth find shelter and peace.

Thank you, God, for this new home.

The New School

Lord, please bless my children as they set off for this new school.

Please let their clothes be right, so that they won't feel conspicuous. Give them courage and confidence, God. Let their native gifts and qualities shine through.

I know that you will help them, and I thank you for it now.

Please enter the hearts of all the others they will meet, in the corridors, in the classrooms, on the playground. Let these other people like them, Lord, and make them welcome, please. Let them find friends right away. But don't let them be so eager to be accepted that they make mistakes.

Help them off to a good start, God. With the new teachers and the new friends that are coming into their lives today.

And please help my children as they continue the process of learning.

Give their teachers patience, understanding. And my children comprehension. Help them to catch up on what they may have missed and to be confident of what they already know.

I know that you will be with them. I know that you will protect them. I know that you will bless them on this first important day in this new school.

The Family Vacation

Oh, God, please bless this journey that we are taking. This family vacation.

Bless the car that we are stuffing with our things— tents, luggage, fishing tackle, toys, games, lunches, thermos jugs. May it be equal to its contents; may its tires be tough and sure, its engine steady and strong. May it carry us safely to our planned destinations.

Thank you for this car, God.

And bless the people who are piling in.

Let their enthusiasm last, at least for the first few

miles. Don't let too many quarrels erupt in the back seat. Let there be enough puzzles and games to keep them occupied when the scenery palls.

Let them be obedient to their father and helpful when it's time to unload. Give them a reasonable measure of kindness and generosity to each other.

Though I realize all this is probably an awful lot to ask, I do ask it and thank you in advance (just in case!).

God, I pray that I've remembered to put in the necessary things. And if I haven't that you'll lead us to the places where we can get them without too much trouble or expense.

Pray too that you will guide us to the right places to stay. Clean, attractive places everybody will enjoy.

Thank you for all the places we will be, and all the things we will see. But most of all that we have a family to take vacationing. And that we are able to go. Free to follow the roads and highways that ribbon this great country, to explore its sights and its cities.

The freedom to travel, God—how we take it for granted, yet what a precious thing it is. Thank you that we can pack up and take off on this adventure, a family vacation trip.

Escape

Listen, Lord, please listen . . .

Forgive me, but it's so good to get away by myself. To have to think only about the clothes I'm going to take. To have to pack nobody's suitcases but my own.

It's even a relief to say good-bye to the family,

disloyal as that sounds. For I know that *you* know
how desperately I need to escape for a while, and
that you'll look after them. That in some ways they
will be better off for my going.

Dear God, how good it is to board a plane and not
feel guilty about taking the window seat. To read to
myself, think my own thoughts, be myself for a
change. To gather myself together as a person, bliss-
fully a stranger among strangers, utterly on my own.

How good it is for me to have to see about luggage,
taxis and all the other complexities of traveling without somebody else along. To register at a hotel and
soak up the unaccustomed luxury. To go into dining
rooms and choose what I want to eat. Or recklessly
phone for room service (a mother *earns* it—after all
the room service she gives at home).

Thank you for this vacation from demanding
voices. From housekeeping and neighbors and tele-
phones. From problems with husband, children, job.

You know I'm glad I have them to go back to, God.
But right now I'm like a new person, someone more
attractive, self-reliant, more interesting even to myself. Someone I need to reclaim.

Thank you for giving me this break, and please let
every woman have one now and then. A chance to
get away, to take a trip alone.

On Having Breakfast In
A Beautiful Hotel

Here I am, God, surrounded by other people in this beautiful hotel.

The carpet is soft, the service swift, the silver and glasses shining. And my heart shines, too, simply at being here.

Thank you for this little hour of luxury before beginning my day. That for a short time I am not in a cluttered kitchen cooking for other people, but that I can sit in peace and have my breakfast brought to me.

Thank you for the chill tomato juice with its slice of lemon, and for the gardens and the tree from which they came. Thank you for the bacon and eggs, the toast, the jam; the coffee hot in its delicate cup. For the morning paper beside my plate.

But most of all for the pleasant murmur of people about me:

The businessmen far from home. The vacationing family. The young couple, still rosy and rapt, wearing their look of wonder. And the old couple to whom wonder is a stranger—yet he holds her chair, butters her toast, and the bond between them has a loveliness all its own.

Bless these people as they face the day. Bless their journeys, whatever direction they go.

Bless all of us, Lord, on our long mysterious journeys that lead us to so many nights, and so many

mornings—so few of them in the peace and charm of
a beautiful hotel.

Flying Through Fog

I can barely see the wings, Lord, but they are
outspread like arms. Like your everlasting arms.

They hold us up, they reach out like a benediction.
"Don't be afraid," they say, and so do the bright little
lights. "We are strong, we are firm."

I see the small flaps open and close as we speed
steadily forward through the fog. They are like the
movements of an enigmatic but reassuring smile.

I am relaxed, I am calm. Who can fear the clouds
and the fog which surround us like the very breath of
God?

Like homing pigeons we are being led to our destination. Blindly yet surely the instruments lead us
home.

Your hand is upon us, your eye is upon us. Though
we rise and fall with the currents—on this journey or
through the fogs of life, you will hold us up. You will
see us through.

We reach firm ground, we land.

Oh, Lord, let me remember this later, at the times
when I need it, when the fogs of life overtake me and
there seems to be no landing place—let me remember
this flight through the fog.

The Woman Within

Hear, O Lord, when I cry with my voice: have mercy also upon me, and answer me.

PSALM 27:7

For My Own Existence

Whatever my pleas and prayers and supplications, Lord, I am thankful just—to be.

That out of the dark mystery of nonexistence, the priceless secret stuff of life was gathered to fashion—me.

That for a little span of time there is upon this planet a person who bears my name, sees with my eyes, feels with my fingers, has my work, my associations, my memories.

Thank you for my emotions, good or bad—joy or despair, hope, happiness, even anxiety.

Thank you for my thoughts. That within my head there is this marvelous chamber in which I can travel, be entertained, dream, plan. A place in which the whole panorama of human adventure can be played at will.

Thank you for my body, able to perform a woman's tasks. To run a vacuum sweeper, make a bed in the morning, get down on my knees and scrub a floor.

A body that can run after children, catch a bus to work, pound a typewriter, walk home on a crisp evening with an armful of groceries.

A body that can swim, dance, rest, rise, love, ride a bicycle (puffingly). Thankful for it even in times of illness or accident, for it makes me aware of how wonderful it is to be well.

Thank you for my own existence, God. I am grateful just to be.

Control

Oh, God, give me more control.

Over my temper, my impulses, my emotions.

I lash out sometimes without meaning to. I act without thinking. I am too quick to hurt, and be hurt. It is as if a flock of demons lives within me ready to spring into action when least expected, without any direction from me.

Don't let them, Lord. Cool these fires, calm these storms. Rid me of them. Harness me with patience and good judgment so that I will be in charge. Give me control.

Oh, Lord give me control—over the people I am responsible for.

I hate to nag, I hate to boss, and I feel so helpless when they refuse to do what they should. Worse, I feel as if I have failed them.

Strengthen my resolve, Lord. Make me more firm, more consistent. Give me more control.

Dear Lord, give me more control over my life.

It is so fragmented, going so many directions. I waste too much time on too many projects, too many people. I work so hard and don't always see results. My real abilities seem forsaken.

There is so little peace and time and quiet in which to sort out values, get perspective. So little time to get to really know myself, or you.

Lord, please give me control over all this. Give me the wisdom and power to be truly in charge of *me*.

Why Am I So Anxious?

Why am I so anxious, Lord? Of what am I afraid?

My anxieties are nameless and elusive; I cannot track down their true source. Yet it is as if dark threats were pressing up from within, hovering like dread birds about me.

Is it the state of the world that disturbs me? Is it the swift passing of time?

Help me to realize that I can't reform the world and I can't save it from its mistakes. I can only do my best to make it a kinder, fairer, more beautiful place wherever I am.

As for time, it has neither end nor beginning. For me as for everyone else, there is only today.

Is it death, is it danger that troubles me?

But life has always been full of danger, and no danger was ever forestalled by anxiety. While to die to this existence is to live in a larger dimension, to possess eternity.

Lord, forgive me for these anxieties that are so at odds with faith. Let me know with my inmost spirit as well as my intelligence that your plan for all mankind includes peace and protection for me.

Don't Let Me Be So Hard On Myself

Father, please don't let me be so impatient with myself.

I fret, I scold, I deplore my many shortcomings.

Why am I so messy? Why do I get myself into such complicated situations? Now why did I say *that?* Won't I ever learn?

My mind carries on an idiot monologue of self-reproach. Or I lie awake bewailing the day's mistakes. I wince before them. I call myself names I would never call other people. I am stung and tormented by these self-lacerations.

I know all this is useless. The more I berate myself the worse I seem to become.

And it gets between us. It is unworthy of the trust I should have in you who made me as I am, and who loves me despite my faults.

I know that you want me to be aware of them and to improve as best I can. But help me to forgive myself a little quicker, to be a little kinder to myself.

To Balance The Scales Of Hurt

Listen, Lord, please listen . . .

Right now I am deeply hurt, and all I can think

about is how to strike back. Please don't let me. Erase from my mind this blind desire to hurt in return.

Isn't there enough hurt in the world already? Let me never add to it no matter how justified I feel.

I have already added my portion of pain. Consciously or unconsciously I too have wounded and disappointed people. Whether I wanted to or not I have done my share, so don't let me come whimpering to you now.

When you told us to love our enemies, to pray for those who persecute us, to return good for evil, you were giving us the toughest assignment of all.

We think we still want the old law—an eye for an eye, a tooth for a tooth (and a tongue for a tongue). But I'm beginning to see that you were right. If that law were really to work, what an awful harvest each of us might reap.

Lord, I don't know whether any of the people I've hurt ever prayed for me or blessed me. But I do know that most of them must have forgiven me. Those who had loved me still do. And little though I deserve it, I could never count their kindness.

Because of that forgiveness, give me the strength to forgive my enemies now. Because of that love, to love them. Because of that goodness, to discover the thrilling reward of returning good for evil.

Bless my enemies. Show me a way to help them. This too is justice.

I Am So Depressed

I am depressed, God. So depressed I'm a little scared.

My heart is literally heavy within me, like a dark weight beating. My whole body is dark and heavy with despair.

I lift up my eyes to your sun and am not consoled. It only seems to burn me.

I hold out my hands to your cool rain when it comes; yet it only chills me.

I look upon my life and am appalled at what seems to me its waste. My failures taunt me. My successes have turned to ashes bitter in my mouth.

The world and its people repel me. I am bereft of warmth and love. Nothing seems to matter anymore.

Forgive me, God, but it's just not worth it.

Oh, Lord, help me. Hang onto me. Don't ask me to be strong right now; only help me to survive.

Remind me that this too will pass. The world will look different tomorrow. Or day after tomorrow.

Love and hope and joy and challenge do return. Glorious things that I will care about intensely. Experiences I couldn't bear to miss.

Thank you for this assurance. With you I can endure. I can bear this depression until it lifts.

The Little Sins

The only sins that deeply trouble me, Lord, are my lesser sins.

Sins of unkindness. Sins of a foolish tongue. Times when I might have helped someone and didn't. Sins of neglect, when I was too busy to be bothered, or simply forgot.

Sins of selfishness. Sins of intolerance. Sins of snap judgments. Sins of stubbornness.

The cruel sins of lost temper and injustice to a child.

Lord, the larger sins don't trouble me so much. Big bold sins I can bring to you with a mighty passion, and through your blood be cleansed.

No, it is the little sins that hover in the background of my life, rising to assault me when least expected. To whine in my ears like insects, to bore into my flesh, to sting.

Pry their petty fingers from my soul. Still their nagging voices; release me from their power to make me wince.

Too small to remember, too many to count, almost too shameful to admit—please purge me of them, Lord. Give me freedom from them—my lesser sins.

These Little Hells

These hells, Lord, these little hells through which we grope.

Help us to see their purpose. Help us to find some meaning in these tormenting fires—some reason, some sense, some hope.

For surely nothing is put upon us that we cannot bear. No suffering that we cannot use—either to help ourselves or others when their time comes to be tested.

Lord, if this be purging, let us know it so that we can more quietly submit.

If this be strengthening, let our feeble powers toughen and be forged afresh.

If this be simply our turn at walking in the common fires of human suffering, let us accept that too without too much complaint. Let us remember how many good people have walked here before us and call up some of the courage they have shown.

But oh, Lord, help us to see the purpose in these little hells life has for us.

Trouble

When I am in trouble I call upon the Lord and he hears me. He listens with an understanding heart.

There is no interruption when I pour forth all my problems. He does not intrude. He does not argue. He does not lecture or scold.

The Lord waits quietly upon my frantic recital, and gradually I feel his peace descending upon me so that I am not distraught or despairing any more.

I become calm when I turn to the Lord in times of trouble. My trials begin to seem of less consequence than I thought. My problems don't seem so hopeless, after all.

Someone stronger than I am is helping me to bear them. A wiser mind than mine is concerned.

I am never alone when I call upon the Lord. In him I find my comfort, my solutions and my strength.

For Tears

I am grateful, God, for tears. For the ability to cry.

How marvelously you made us that we are equipped with this way to express our emotions.

Quick tears to relieve the sudden hurt. Or for the times when we are touched, too moved to speak.

Or when deeper sorrows come, that we have this fierce and wonderful cleansing. This release that helps to wash away the very grief our crying demonstrates.

How you must love us that you thus provided for us. No other being has it, no insect, bird or beast. Only man and woman made in your likeness.

We are the only creatures who can cry.

Jesus wept, as we weep. Our very tears are testimony to your fatherhood. We too are your sons and daughters.

Thank you for this proof, and for this healing outlet, the ability to cry.

For Laughter

Thank you, Lord, for laughter.

And for all the people who can bring it about, make us see the funny side of things.

The world is so full of anguish; life itself sometimes seems so grim. Thank you that in your vast understanding you gave us laughter to make us forget, to restore our wounded spirits, brighten the journey, lighten the load.

Just as you saved tears for human beings, you blessed us alone with laughter.

And surely this too is a clue to your very nature. A nature akin to our own.

Thank you for this blessing, Lord. This shining gift of laughter.

Open The Channel

God, help me to stop trying to fit you into the framework of my desires.

Let me stop exhorting and demanding and even scheming to try to mold your will to mine.

Instead, help me to be a channel for the bounty of your blessings. Cleanse me of the dark broodings that dim the light of your presence. Rid me of the clutter of my doubts.

For then, only then, are you able to pour into my life the rich rewards you are prepared to give.

Lord, shape me, mold me, purify and ease me so that I am able to receive.

Woman on Trial

O God, thou knowest my foolishness; and my sins are not hid from thee.

PSALM 69:5

The Aged Parent

One

My father has come to live with us, Lord. And we love him. We tell him, and ourselves, that we want him. But it is hard, so hard on all of us.

Nobody is interested in his stories, which we've heard so often. He gets in the way when company is here. He gets underfoot in the kitchen. He drops things, spills things. He broke my favorite dish and I had to bite my tongue. He was so contrite, so pathetic trying to mend it.

His hands shake, Lord. Those dear hands that worked so hard for us.

He gets out his wallet or his old-fashioned snap purse and gives the children money, though I've asked him not to. He can't afford it, and it isn't good for them.

Then I remember when those hands were strong and proud, the source of plenty. I remember when he was a hero to us, as he wants to be a hero to my children. I see how those hands tremble and I can't stand it.

My father, my own dear father, Lord. And I simply don't have time for him.

I urge him to go play shuffleboard, and hate myself as he trudges obediently down the walk like a child shooed outdoors. And he comes back all too soon. There are many old ladies who enjoy each other's company, but there aren't many old men. And he

doesn't want to be with them anyway. Those weeks
he was ill he clung to me so eagerly.

I am haunted by the specter of a long illness, Lord.
He is so plainly stricken at the prospect of a nursing
home, and they are so expensive. How could we pay
for it if the time should come when we'd be forced to
send him?

Sometimes, forgive me, I think of the unfairness of
this burden when we still have our family to think of.

Our family ... just as he once had *his*. To support,
to break his back for without complaining. And not
only us—he was so good to his father and mother.
Oh, God, when I think I can't endure this, let me
remember how good he was to my grandparents.

How can I even speak of fairness if I complain at
my turn to take care of the father who took care of all
of us so long, and did it with so much less?

Dear Lord, please let the deep love and gratefulness I have for my father be paramount. Let it fill
me, guide me, help me to triumph over these personal
conflicts.

Two

My father is so lonely, Lord. Give me compassion.
Give me understanding. Help me to ease his loneliness.

He often sits silent, gazing into the distance, and I
know he is thinking of Mother. Remembering the
days when he and she too were young and vigorous
and important. But mostly just—missing Mother.

And my heart breaks for him. I am bloody with
guilt and self-reproach ... And awe.

For I see him as the true source of me. This man
whose intense love for her brought me into existence.
Too often I reject him, fret about him—and yet here

he is, one secret of my being. One answer to my eternal question.

Who am I? I am child of my father. This father under my roof, close enough to touch.

His sperm gave me life, his blood gave me substance, his genes gave me individuality. His strong daily living example helped to shape the person I have become.

Oh, dear heavenly father, thank you for this father made in your image here on earth. For giving me this opportunity to know him, love him, revere him. To make his final days as pleasant as possible before he goes to join her. His wife, my mother, the woman he loved so much.

Three

Lord, help us to realize that we too will one day be old, with our life's work over, our responsibilities behind us, many of our best friends gone. And to start preparing for it now.

Give us such a vast and varied range of interests that we will never need anyone to entertain us or be at a loss how to fill our days. Now, when we're still strong and healthy, let us take the best possible care of our bodies, so we will be less subject to the debilities of age.

Keep us from laziness, Lord. From making excuses for ourselves. Help us to remember that we can always do the things we enjoy so long as we don't *stop* doing them.

But let us design some plan so that should the time come when we can no longer care for ourselves, we won't have to live with younger people who are too busy for us.

Meanwhile, help us to be kind, oh, very patient

and kind to older people, who have merely reached a
plateau of life where we too will be someday.

To Witness Suffering

Oh, God, this suffering ... to be helpless witness to
another person's suffering.

It seems that my own I could bear more easily. At
least I could cry out lustily, bloodily. I could wrestle
it, fight it, put up a mighty battle.

But this—to be whole and strong, every sense vivid
and vulnerable, and be forced to attend a loved one's
agony. To hear the cries and witness the struggle yet
be powerless to put an end to it.

Or to have to be brave because the sufferer is so
brave. To be cheerful when the heart is breaking. To
live within sight and sound and touch of the endless
suffering, essential to the victim's very existence.

I cry out against this sometimes, Lord. Even as I
beg deliverance for the sufferer, or that some of these
torments be put upon me instead. Why do you allow
it? What earthly good is such suffering? And why
have I been cast in this role?

Then I realize that you are not the author of
suffering, but that you alone can take our suffering
and turn it to some good purpose. What that purpose
is I don't know, only that it *is*.

Surely for that reason you made me unusually
strong, resilient, enduring. Able to comfort if only by
not breaking down. Able to share some modicum of
that strength.

Lord, when I think I can endure this no longer, let me remember those who did not flee the scene of the cross.

Help me to keep my vigil with suffering as courageously as they kept theirs.

Divorce

"What God has joined together, let no man put asunder," the commandment goes. And when that commandment is broken, whatever the justification, there is bound to be pain.

Lord, please help all the people who must suffer through this divorce. Don't let any of us lose faith in ourselves, in each other, or in you.

There's no use going into all the complex reasons that brought about this tragedy—you know them only too well.

But now that the severing must and will take place, ease the pain, heal the wounds. Let your great love flow through the lives of everyone concerned, washing away remorse, regrets, recriminations, bitter memories.

Through the miracle of that love let all the people love each other in a new way. Let there be genuine forgiveness. Let there be genuine hope for the happiness of each other.

Oh, God, may the very pain of this divorce perform a mighty purging, so that we will all be better people in the end.

The Blessings Of Injury

Thank you, Lord, for the unexpected blessings of this injury.

Now that the pain has abated, now that the sense of protest and sheer frustration is over, I can see that it is really doing me good.

From this strange vantage point of almost comic immobility I can comprehend the rat race from which I was forced to withdraw. I can marvel at some of the futility, the sheer waste-motion.

When I return to it I believe I will be better able to function smoothly, effectively.

And I will appreciate the sheer wonder of being able to walk, run up and downstairs, dance, kick, swim.

I have learned humility, Lord. I have learned patience.

I have learned consideration and compassion for others who are forced into the indignity of casts and crutches and wheelchairs. I will be more thoughtful of them, more helpful—as people have been to me.

I have learned how kind and generous and good people can be.

Thank you for these blessings. Thank you for the lessons I have learned from this injury.

The Twilight Zone

This person who is so dear to me is lost to me, Lord.

He is with me and yet not with me. He is in some twilight zone of drink or drugs or sickness of the mind that makes him speak strangely, act strangely; there is a lost inhuman look in his eyes.

I am terrified for him, Lord, and for myself. I don't know what he might do, or what *I* might do. For my emotions are an intolerable mixture of tenderness and detestation. I am being torn apart in an agony of love.

He is so terribly lonely, wherever he is. And I . . . I too am in limbo, forced to wander in an unspeakable loneliness.

Help me, oh Lord, help me. I am so bewildered. I can't call him back to my presence. I don't even know what to do when the awfulness has passed.

Help me to remember that this is an illness, a tragic illness of body and spirit. Give me patience, give me compassion, give me the strength to endure this, and when it is over give me judgment.

He needs help so badly, but I don't know where to turn. You must guide me, you must direct me to those who can help us. You must give me faith in them and in you.

Meanwhile, thank you that you have not abandoned me. I am not really alone even in these terrible times when he is lost to me.

You are sustaining me, and when he is himself you will give me the strength and wisdom to restore him to sanity and health.

I've Got To Stop Smoking

I've got to stop smoking, God. But how? How?

I've read the books about it, taken the courses, tried all the remedies from candy substitutes to pills. But nothing helps. I crave the very enslavement from which I long to be freed. My body craves it, my psyche craves it—the hot comfort of the same insidious enemy that is destroying me.

I know the damage it's doing my body. I know the bad example it's setting for my children. For the sake of their bodies if not my own, for the sake of their future peace of mind and self-respect, please help me.

Lord, I can't lick this battle without you.

You, who created my body in the first place, healthy and untainted, give me the moral strength to restore that healthy body now.

I claim your power to sweep this poison from my bloodstream, purify my lungs. I claim your power to shake this awful dependence from my soul. I claim your ability to make me proud of myself again instead of guilty and ashamed.

You will stay my hand when it reaches for the source of my misery; you will give me the will to cast it away. During the hours of torment while I struggle to refrain, the peace of your presence will fill me.

I feel it now as I pray. I know its comfort, its

reassurance. With you beside me I am no longer
vulnerable, I am in complete control.

Thank you, Lord, that this time I shall succeed.

I've Got To Lose Weight

Problems of the flesh are hard to pray about. They
seem so—almost unworthy, compared to others.

But the doctor tells me I've got to lose weight,
Lord. And it's no surprise; the mirror's been telling
me the same thing.

You know my laziness, my reluctance to admit the
truth.

You know my bad habits. How I often eat not
because my body needs sustenance, but only because
I'm bored or restless or filled with uncertainties. To
fill the time, to comfort myself, to feed my hungry
heart.

Now, with your help, this is going to stop.

You will give me the will and the self-discipline to
stick to this diet. You will fill me with spiritual food
so nourishing, so delightful and satisfying that I won't
be tempted (well ... too unbearably tempted) to
break faith with myself.

You will feed me what I need to have, just as you
fed your early followers.

Come to think of it, I don't imagine there were any
fat martyrs or any fat saints. Certainly there couldn't
have been any fat disciples walking the roads with
their master, never sure of where their next meal was
coming from.

You know I don't care to be a martyr or a saint,

Lord. (Though I'll *feel* like a martyr as I try, and certainly feel like a saint when I succeed.) But I do aspire to be your disciple—a modern, slender one.

With your help I know I can make it. Thank you, Lord.

Is It Right For Me?

I am being asked to do something that goes against my principles, Lord.

It will harm nobody, I'm assured, and greatly benefit me.

I'd be a fool not to take advantage of it, I'm told. It's done all the time by perfectly respectable people who don't see anything wrong with it. Who, in fact, can produce all sorts of reasons for considering it right.

Just as I'm able to rationalize it myself. Able to justify it. I really deserve the money involved and I certainly could use it. Not only for myself but for others. I could compensate for the guilt I already feel. I could do a lot of good with that money.

Nobody could get hurt. Nobody else would know.

Only me . . . And you.

That's the trouble, Lord. It's hurting already. It goes against the grain of my deeper self. Something within me writhes. Yet I'm no better than other people; if it's right for them why isn't is right for me?

Even this indecision is hurting. For no matter what logic I use to convince myself, it sounds shallow and false when I present it like this to you. And I know if

I yield to this temptation I will feel estranged from you.

This, surely this is the answer. Nothing is worth that price. Thank you for giving me the strength to do what I know is right for me.

The Attraction

I am intensely attracted to this man, God, and he is attracted to me. We sensed it the instant we met. There was a shock of recognition, as if we already understood each other and had many things to say to each other, many things to share.

It is a dear anguish to be in the same room, so overpowering is our desire to look at each other, seek each other out, speak, touch. The longing to explore the exciting mystery of the other.

But he is not free and I am not free. To pursue this attraction to its logical end would hurt many people. Hurt, perhaps ruin, the very thing that seems so rare and wonderful now.

Yet I yearn for this man, Lord. Blindly, selfishly, I want to be with him. I feel like a lovesick adolescent who has nothing to go on but his emotions.

Don't let me behave like one. Don't let me do anything foolish. Help me to use my adult intelligence and experience and act accordingly.

God, give me perspective on this strong attraction.

It is no discredit to our partners. There are many fascinating people in the world, but when we marry we must make a choice. The promise to forsake all others, no matter how enticing, is a safeguard against those we are bound to meet—otherwise your world would be one whale of a mess.

Yet attractions like this can still happen—simply because we are human. And it takes will power to resist. It takes strength of character and self-control. It also takes simple old-fashioned loyalty and fair play. And common sense.

I call upon you to fortify these qualities in me now. I claim your help in not allowing myself to be drawn into temptation or futile daydreaming about this man.

But don't let me feel guilty about this attraction either, Lord.

Our time upon earth is short, and rapport between individuals, however briefly sensed, both sweet and rare. Don't let me decry it. Even as I forgo it, don't let me despoil its loveliness by being ashamed of it.

Surely anything that makes us more acutely aware of another human being or arouses such feelings of joy and wonder isn't evil.

It has made me feel newly alive, Lord. More beautiful. More gloriously a woman. More gay and tender with the children. Capable of more generously loving my husband—and understanding him.

So I know you will forgive me when I confess that I feel this intense attraction. And understand when I thank you for it.

Have I Really Failed?

I'm afraid I've failed you, God. I haven't made the most of the talent you gave me. I haven't lived up to my true potential.

I have taken care of people who needed me, and this I don't regret. This too was your scheme of life for me. But I am racked with guilt for the waste of my abilities. For the time squandered on meaningless pleasures, people who mean nothing to me, meaningless pursuits.

Looking back, I am sick with the way I've mismanaged my life. The foolish choices, the opportunities missed. I didn't take all the wrong roads, but far too many. Alluring little paths that turned out to lead no place. Deadend streets from which I discovered, too late, there was not even any backing away.

Forgive me, God, for botching it all up so. But forgive me, maybe even more, for getting so depressed about it. I know I have a lot, such a lot, to be thankful for. And I have accomplished quite a bit compared to many others.

But that isn't the comparison that counts. I am disappointed in *me*.

Lord, deliver me from this disappointment.

If I must look back, let me see that I did the best I could under the circumstances. That I learned things I needed to know, even from seemingly futile experiences. That it was at least in part, a time of testing. (Don't let me alibi, Lord, but let me be fair to myself too.)

So have I really failed you? Have I really failed?

Rescue me, God, from this grieving over the past. Free me to focus my energies and the abilities you gave me on today.

Help me to realize that the soul's true success lies in you. Now that I have found you and am willing to use my gifts as you wish, I have not really failed.

The Best Of My Life

Listen, Lord . . .
I sometimes feel so futile. As if the best of my life
is over and there is no place for me anymore.

My husband doesn't depend on me the way he did.
He no longer needs the encouragement I could give
him as a young man making his way. I don't have to
be nice to his boss anymore, entertain the way I used
to, be a credit to him. Physically and emotionally his
needs are different.

He's made his mark and there's nothing to strive for
anymore.

The children are grown. Nobody needs me for car
pools or dancing lessons or scout trips or conferences
at school. Things I used to fret about. But now that
they're over I feel bewildered. Instead of relief, there
is this emptiness and sense of loss. Particularly since
they are too busy to notice. They hardly ever write
and seldom call, and I'm too fearful of being a bother
to let them know.

I don't even feel as important in my community or
my work anymore. Younger women are taking over.
And despite their inexperience, doing an excellent
job.

I don't resent them, Lord, don't really envy them.
And yet I feel displaced, as if all my years of faithful
service haven't really meant very much in the final
analysis.

Listen, Lord, please help me snap out of this mood

of self-pity and inutility. Bestir me, shake me—wake me up to a sense of excitement again at the challenge of the day. The sheer wonder of having time at last available to try formerly impossible things.

Remind me that there's so much to learn about the world and the unmet needs of thousands of other people everywhere. Not only can I take courses, I can teach courses for people who want what I already know.

Needed? Oh, Lord, make me realize that so long as there is a lonely, hungry, troubled or underprivileged person on this earth I *am* needed, desperately. And in meeting even a small portion of their need I will become important once more, I will be replenished and fulfilled.

Thank you, God, for showing me that the best of my life is far from over; perhaps the richest, most satisfying part is only about to begin.

Woman Alone

I call to remembrance my song in the night: I commune with mine own heart.

PSALM 77:6

This Hurt

Listen, Lord, please listen ...

You will help me to bear this hurt. This seemingly intolerable pain.

You will help me not to cry out in agony. But you will be patient with me too; you will not ask me to be too brave inside.

This hurt, oh God, this hurt.

It is a shock, it dazes and numbs me. So that for a little while I can move blindly, almost insensate, about my duties.

Then it revives, it comes again in waves, rhythmic beatings that seem almost not to be borne. Yet I know that I must bear them, as a woman endures the pains of birth.

I am in labor, Lord. A terrible labor of the spirit. And it is infinitely worse than childbirth because right now I can see no deliverance. And I will have nothing to show for it.

Or—will I? Will I, Lord?

Surely I will have new strength in compensation. Surely somewhere inside me there will be some hard sustaining residue, some accretion of anguish like the mineral deposits from water, or rocks hardened out of a volcano's boiling lava.

Perhaps this very pain is building a rock cliff within me that will stand stern against further assaults of pain and grief. And it will be both a protection and a base from which to start anew.

Thank you for this revelation. You who are truly the "rock of ages" will support me and help to build in me this other rock of strength.

When Loneliness Is New

Loneliness is so new to me, Lord. I need your help in handling it.

Help me to be a little more proud. Not aloof, but a little less eager for human contact. Let me remember that other people are busy with their friends and families. Don't let me overwhelm them with invitations.

I don't want them to feel obliged to come, out of concern for me. And certainly under no obligation to "do something for me" in return.

This is a delicate area, Lord—help me to handle it sensibly and cheerfully.

Please guide me too when it comes to accepting invitations.

My loneliness is sometimes so acute I feel I'd go almost anywhere at any time with anybody. This an affront to my self-respect.

Don't let me be too proud, too choosy, but don't let my desperation show or get me into situations I'd regret.

Lord, help me not to talk too much when I do go out. Especially about myself—my problems, my grief.

Let me remember how I've dreaded seeing other lonely women who pinion people to hear their tales of woe. Don't let me cheapen my sorrow by wearing it on my sleeve.

Lord, make me good company, so that people still want me for myself.

Help me to remember that I'm not the first person to face loneliness, and I won't be the last. Thank you that talking to you about it will help me to handle it gracefully.

The Lonely Women

God bless lonely women.

All lonely women who come home at night to find no man there.

No scent of smoke lingering. No ashtrays overflowing. No exasperation of men's dear strewings—socks, papers, coins, keys. No sweet tang of shaving lotion and cigars.

God bless all lonely women who will not leap at the sound of a strong male step on the stairs.

God bless women, all the lonely women who lie mateless in the night, hungry for the comfort of arms around them. A strong shoulder to rest on (and cry on and complain on). A male presence to depend on, sensible or brave when threatening noises pierce the dark.

God bless women without men to solve things, fix things, find things—bills and problems and toasters and washing machines and missing fuses so there will be light.

Women who have no man to zip them up, repair an

earring, run an errand, share a hope, a dream, a memory, a surprise.

God be gentle with women who have loved men, lost men, or missed the marvel of being with men.

And put gentleness in the hearts of all women who still have men—that they may be kinder to the lonely women, and infinitely more kind to the men who share their lives.

This Loneliness

This loneliness, Lord. This blind blank terror of loneliness.

These days and nights when nobody speaks or comes near and the telephone doesn't ring. This near-panic at times, when it seems that nobody knows I exist.

See me through, give me moral courage. Don't let me feel so sorry for myself. Don't let me blame people for what seems cruel neglect. (Remind me to be fair. This is a couple's society, and I wasn't much concerned about the plight of unattached women before.)

Stay very close to me. Comfort me. Fill me with a sense of your presence. Let me learn to savor solitude as a long-sought chance to draw nearer to you.

But oh, Lord, remember that I'm human too. In this world and very much of it.

You made us of flesh and blood with a consuming need for the sight and sound and touch of our own kind. Restore me to avenues of human contact. Show me ways to enter the mainstream of life once more.

She Sits In Darkness

I thought I was lonely, Lord, until I found this woman.

She is blind, quite blind; she sits alone in the darkness.

She is deaf, quite deaf; she sits alone in the silence.

She is ill, quite ill; it is difficult for her to move.

I cannot speak to her, I cannot let her know who I am. I can only press her hand and try to comfort her by my presence, so that she will not feel quite so alone.

Lord, I know now what loneliness is. I have been in its presence. I know that I am not truly lonely, after all.

I can see—I have the company of magazines and books.

I can hear—I have the company of my radio, my telephone, my TV set.

I can move, Lord. I can go about my work, my errands, and go to call on this woman.

"Who am I?" I have often asked of you, and of myself. How much more this question must torment anyone lost in the silent darkness.

I must help her to find an answer to that question. I must let her know, somehow, that she is real and important. Very important. Very real.

She has deeply touched another human being. And because of her I am less lonely and less lost!

God, convey this to her. Help me to make her aware of this.

I'm So Sick Of Women

Oh, God, dear God, I'm so hungry for a man.

A man to hold me, a man's body warm against mine, a man's arms around me. A man to protect me, cherish me, comfort me. A man to talk to, and even to fight with sometimes.

I'm so sick of women.

Sick of the smell and sight and sound of women, compensating for the emptiness by gossip and bridge and concerts and fashion shows.

I seek out their company yes, just as they seek mine. I am grateful for it. Yet there is something vital missing when women huddle together for social protection, like sheep.

We go home only faintly comforted, vaguely appeased.

I long for a man's footsteps, a man's big rough coat in the closet, even the clutter of a man's things around. I long for the sound and scent of a man, sweaty from golf, greasy from fixing a car, singing in the shower.

Not just any man, Lord. A good strong man, a man I can respect.

Surely somewhere there is such a man. Someone as lonely as I am, as hungry for companionship.

Bless him wherever he is and lead him toward me. Help us to find each other.

(And oh, bless and help all my lonely sisters who, like me, are secretly seeking a man.)

Not Just Any Man

Listen, Lord, please listen ...

Please don't think me too preoccupied with finding a man. It can't be just any man.

Selfish though it may seem, I don't want a weak, ailing man who expects me to nurse him the rest of his life. Or to be a companion and nurse to his aged mother. Or to pay his bills. Or to raise a difficult child while he's off traveling.

You know I'd do any of these things willingly, joyfully, for a man who truly loved me and whom I loved. Who put our relationship first, and proved it, long before these other responsibilities came along.

But these misfits who've never married, or made a botch of it. Who are simply seeking a woman to lean on. Forgive me, but I'm not *that* lonely.

God, please don't think me too self-centered. Too independent or hard to please.

But guard me against desperation. Help me to live forever in my loneliness if need be, before I rush into some foolish relationship with just any man.

The Lovely Solitude

I've just come from visiting a big noisy family and I'm exhausted. Filled with happy memories yes, but glad to get home.

And now seems a good time to realize that instead of lamenting my loneliness, I should be singing the blessings of solitude!

Thank you for silence, Lord. Sheer silence can indeed be golden. And so can order. I gaze about this apartment with new respect; it seems beautiful right now, and simple to keep it so with nobody to pick up after but myself.

And independence—how divine. The freedom to do what I please.

I can listen to the kind of music I really enjoy or watch the kind of television shows. I can read, write, sew, paint or just think without being interrupted.

I can read in bed at night as late as I want without disturbing anybody. I don't have to worry about anybody else's feelings, or have my own unexpectedly hurt. I don't have to argue or pretend to agree when I don't.

I don't have to be bored. I can give a party. I can call up a friend for lunch.

And even if all the people I know are busy, I have only to dial a few numbers, travel a few blocks to be in the thick of those who'll welcome me with open arms. My clubs, my church—hospitals, the Y, the Salvation Army.

More places than I can count, where there are always vital, joyous, stimulating people; and people whose loneliness and needs so far surpass mine that I feel richly endowed and aglow.

Lord, let me remember all this when loneliness gets me down.

And let me remember it also when I get too enamored with solitude. Don't let me become ingrown and selfish.

There is so much work to be done and so many people to be helped and enjoyed. Especially for the woman who lives alone.

Woman and God

Then said I, Lo, I come: in the volume of the book it is written of me.

PSALM 40:7

Identity

Who am I? Who am I, God?

So many of us have been asking so long. Secretly or openly asking—over the coffee, at our sinks, at our desks, on the subway, on our knees.

Where did I come from, and why? Is this all there is to it?

The grind of it. The cheap little, dear little joys of it. Or the big ones that last so briefly and often must be paid for at such an exorbitant price.

The loneliness, the hurt, the failure. The drudgery, the despair. Even the sweetness, the poignancy, the almost intolerable beauty ... Why?

And who am I that I am thrust into the midst of it, out of no place, seemingly going nowhere?

Sex provides no answers. Jobs provide no answers. Causes provide no answers. Families provide no answers.

Without you there are no answers. We do come from nowhere, live as nobody, die as nobody and vanish into nowhere. We are as anonymous as the Unknown Soldier, or a nameless criminal who lies in an unmarked grave.

All the tags and markers that the world can heap upon us cannot eradicate the futile, eternal mystery.

But with you we do come from somewhere. We are somebody.

Each day that we live, however humbly, we are critically important individuals of your fashioning.

You have given us purpose. Our lives are guided by

your hand. Rich or poor, in joy or suffering, our identity lies in you.

We *are* going somewhere, however we question or quarrel with what happens along the way. You will lead us to the destination you mean for us.

Thank you for this knowledge. I need not question who I am so long as I know that I am one with you.

Psalm For Deliverance

I pleaded with God to deliver me from trouble.

My brain was bruised from seeking solutions. My body ached from the effort. My nerves were strung tight; they would break, I knew, something would break if I forced myself to go on.

"Help me," I kept crying to my God. "Give me answers. Deliver me from this torment." But my own voice seemed to despair of such deliverance even as I called.

Then a strange quiet came upon me. A kind of divine indifference. I knew without words or even thoughts that I could only withdraw and wait quietly upon the Lord.

And he did not forsake me.

He came in the quiet of the night; he was there in the brilliance of the morning. He touched my senses with hope; he healed my despair. And with the awareness of his presence came the deliverance I sought.

The answers would be provided. Quietly, and in God's own way, they were working even as I waited.

Inventory

Listen, Lord, please listen . . .
In all humility, I think I should take inventory.
Thank you that I am not the person I used to be.

As I look back I wince to think of my shallowness,
my false concepts, my blunders. A dismal flock of
faults that there is no use raking over—except to
marvel at how, with your help, I have been able to
overcome them.

Not completely—no. I have fumbled and stumbled
many times, and there is still a long way to go.

But thank you for your love, even when you are
disappointed in me.

Thank you for your patience. Thank you for your
presence, which has steadied me on this journey and
never gives up on me.

I am not gloating, Lord, I am simply grateful.

And because I often despair of myself, I think you
want me to look back sometimes and see my own
progress as a person, too.

When The Heart Is Ready

The rain falls on the just and the unjust. And so
does the sunshine of your being.

Sometimes the cloud of my resentment, my rebellion and my sin shuts you out. Yet the rain still falls upon me, and the sunshine of your concern for me still is all about me.

Whether I am right or wrong, just or unjust, seeking or rejecting, you care about me. I know this, no matter what. Whether I acknowledge it or not, it fortifies me. It is very consoling.

But how much better it is when I lift up my arms to your presence and let these gifts fall full upon me.

My open arms are like wings; they lift and express the openness of my heart. My face is no longer turned away from you, but open, ready.

My very body feels the rain and the sun of your love upon it. I reach out with all my being for your blessing. And receive it—receive it in mighty measure.

For your gifts are abundant and your love without limit when the heart is ready.

The Holy Spirit

I prayed for the Holy Spirit to come into me, Lord.

I prayed for the fullness of its fire, destroying the old proud, rebellious, selfish, foolish me.

And the sweet fire came and I was purged. For a time, for a time, I was freed.

Then the old me roused up scowling and full of darkness and began to misbehave. Yet the memory of the fire remained to comfort me.

I prayed for the Holy Spirit to fill me with its loving ecstasy. I prayed for the gift of its love abiding.

And the Spirit came, it caught my heavy heart and

shook it like a toy, it caused my soul to soar. I kicked off my shoes and danced, like David, to glorify the Lord.

I danced and sang in my newfound bliss and dedicated myself to loving kindness forever. I was changed by its power; for a time I was deeply and markedly changed.

But old habits began to rattle their chains; I felt their dread pulling.

And the world said, "You idiot, not so fast, am I really worth your loving?" And the pain, frustration, disappointment, the sheer confusion and conflicts of living, began to batter the holy joy. To quench the fires and still the singing.

I was angry and confused. I felt betrayed. Yet the memory of the lightness and the loving joy remained.

And no matter how I failed my own vision of myself, or how the world defected, I walked a little more gently, kindly, radiantly for it.

Now I thank you, God, for the baptism of love and fire, which is only the beginning.

For I know now that we cannot dance barefoot forever, or wear our souls naked in the streets. We must walk slowly, hopefully, trustingly, patiently.

But even wearing the same old shoes of self, our step will be lighter, life will be better because it came.

The Radiant Company

The Lord has led me into the radiant company of his people. Praise the Lord.

The Lord has given me the fellowship of others on the selfsame journey to find him.

He has given me a spiritual family. He has given me sisters in the dearest sense of the word. He has given me brothers.

We worship together, work together, pray together. And are as richly rewarded in the praying as those we pray for.

I can worship the Lord alone. I can pray alone.

I can know him fully and completely in total solitude. And this is good. For most of our lives we are alone. Despite the presence of many people, we are alone.

But to pray and worship the Lord with others who earnestly, honestly seek him, is to add new dimensions of strength and joy.

Praise the Lord for this gift of fellowship and friendship. For the miracles of work and happiness and healing that burst like stars and change the course of lives when people come together who truly love the Lord.

For Showing Me Purpose

I am grateful, God, that I have finally come to realize your purpose for me.

Just when or how this came about I can't say. It wasn't sudden and dramatic, the way it happened to Paul on the road to Damascus, or Peter Marshall with his experience on the Scottish moors.

There have been no visions, no voices, no letters written in fire upon a wall saying: "Do this." "Do that." "This is your reason for being."

No, my search for you and for the meaning you had

for my life has been uncertain, groping, erratic, filled with accidents, false goals. Sometimes I seemed to sense that purpose, clearly see it; but it vanished like a mirage in the harried, often cruel business of everyday.

Again I seemed on the very verge of knowing, asserting, driving forward toward it. Only to be diverted, led astray.

Yet somehow you keep track of your floundering creatures.

You never really let go. You pick us up and gently press us forward onto the path of our God-given destinies.

Maybe because life is so filled with defeat and heartbreak, we find ourselves turning to you, yielding ourselves to your will, fighting less furiously for selfish, often empty goals. And when this happens we find that you have turned our sufferings and our failures into little stepping-stones.

Looking back, we see them. These rocks which gradually, all unknown to us, you have been shaping to lead us toward our purpose ... And we have been following! However blindly, however zigzag the course, yet we have been moving toward it.

And looking about, we see there are results. There are signals, heartening little affirmations, unexpected proofs.

And our purpose, that blessed sense of purpose, has become a conviction within us; not suddenly but steadily and in secret, until we realize that it has become a part of us, part of our very breath and bone.

We know, Lord, we simply know that our life has meaning. And what we are meant to do with your precious gift of life if we are to fulfill that meaning.

However humble our circumstances or undramatic our talents, our true purpose has been revealed. We were meant to be this person at this time and place. Not only for ourselves, but for you and other people—we were meant to make this particular contribution to the world.

And so we must do it well. Do it with faith and patience, with all our strength and passion. And in so doing discover who we really are.

Thank you, God, that to anyone who truly seeks, you will reveal your purpose.

For Making Me Whole

You have taken the scattered elements of my life and drawn them together into a meaningful whole. Thank you, Lord.

You have fused them into something significant, something with which I can be content. Of which I can even be proud. Thank you, Lord.

Wife, mother, homemaker, would-be reformer of the world. Professional woman. Woman with a family, or woman starkly alone ... The presence of God is like a great light blurring all these distinctions, forging them into something beautifully sure and serene.

Successes or failures don't matter so much anymore.

For the only success is to become a woman whole and fulfilled in the sight of God. The only failure to fall away, still fighting, still crying out against complex and unjust fate, when to be rescued is only to reach out and hold fast to the hand of God.

You have rescued me from the disaster of my own confusions and regrets. You have hauled me up, dripping and kicking, onto the shining shore.

The great light of your love has warmed me, calmed me, healed the ragged edges, certified my only true role.

I feel the very core of me standing proud and strong. A woman blessed by the very responsibilities you gave me, toughened yet smoothed by the very suffering.

Thank you, God, for gathering me back to you, making me whole.

Myself

Thank you, God, for the dignity and beauty of self.

The precious, innate self. The only thing that can't be taken from us. The only thing we really own.

Not selfishness. Not self-seeking, self-will, self-gain. But the wonder of being, simply being—*oneself*.

God-created, God-watched, God-known.

Accountable, actually, only to you who made us. Shaped each of us outwardly so much alike, and yet made each of us so different in the vital, secret self.

You, who expect of each of us different things. You alone can go all the way with us. Take the final journey with us, and be there when we arrive. You will ask the final accounting of this self and its mission upon the earth.

In knowing you I need no longer question, "Who am I?"

I know. Insofar as it is possible, I know. Through you I know the true dignity, worth and beauty of my own being. For whatever my failings, I am a part of you who made me.

In knowing you, I know myself.